Pure Nostalgia

Pure Nostalgia

MEMORIES OF EARLY IOWA

edited and with introductions by

CARL HAMILTON

The Iowa State University Press / Ames

I·O·W·A
HERITAGE
COLLECTION

CARL HAMILTON was formerly vice-president for information and development, Iowa State University. He was editor of the *Hardin County Times* and *Iowa Falls Citizen* and has received the Iowa Press Association's Master Publisher Award. He is the author of *In No Time at All.*

Manufactured in the United States of America

First edition, 1979
Second printing, 1979
Second paperback edition, 1984
Iowa Heritage Collection edition, 1988

Library of Congress Cataloging-in-Publication Data
Pure nostalgia.

(Iowa heritage collection)
Reprint. Originally published: Ames : Iowa State University Press, 1979.
1. Iowa—Biography.   2. Iowa—Social life and customs.   I. Hamilton, Carl, 1914–   II. Series.
CT234.P87   1988   977.7′02   88–13116
ISBN 0–8138–0977–0

C O N T E N T S

PROLOGUE

WHAT could these Iowans have in common—a country doctor, two farm wives, a country editor, a railroad conductor, a legislator, and a business executive? It is that each of them recorded on a warm, first-person basis the unique experiences they had in a period of American life that has disappeared in the onrush of our nation's development—in that so-called twinkling of an eye. Each of them "engraved" a bit of history found nowhere else. Conventional history books paint with broad brushes; these persons "tell it like it was" on a one-to-one, I-was-there basis.

You will feel the disappointments, the hurts, the heat, the cold, the tears, and the frustrations. But you will sense too the outright laughs. For the jauntiness and poignancy in these stories tell us also of an appealing time now past which we long for and sometimes even try to recreate.

The stories generally concern experiences during the latter half of the last century and that part of this century which ended—dismally—with the Depression years. The time covered is roughly 1850-1940.

So most readers will find them pure nostalgia—as well as pure delight.

These pieces all came to my desk after the appearance of *In No Time At All* (Iowa State University Press, 1974) which was itself a bit of nostalgia. In most cases these little essays represent only excerpts from privately printed books or articles which the authors or their representatives have kindly granted us permission to use.

No doubt the publisher will feel obligated to attach my name to this effort in some way. That will bring me a feeling of guilt for the "work" was all put forth on the part of others. Reading and selecting was a pure joy. Deciding what had to be eliminated was dismaying; so much that was so good was left on the cutting room floor. But I had some fine assistance. As was the case with *In No Time At All,* Kay Boyington typed and retyped and kept track of all the things the editor was constantly losing. No small assignment. And also for the second time around, Rowena Malone, senior editor at the Iowa State University Press, brought good sense and a fine professional editor's touch to the manuscript which made this an immeasurably better book than it would otherwise have been. To them my very great thanks.

Aside from deletions, no changes have been made in the texts except to regularize minor punctuation, and to occasionally modernize or correct spellings.

As was the case with *In No Time At All,* I am assigning the royalties from the sale of this book to the Iowa State University Achievement Fund. Regardless how the book strikes your fancy, give it as gifts, urge it on your friends; the royalties go for a good cause.

CARL HAMILTON

Pure Nostalgia

LOVINGLY SUBMITTED . . .

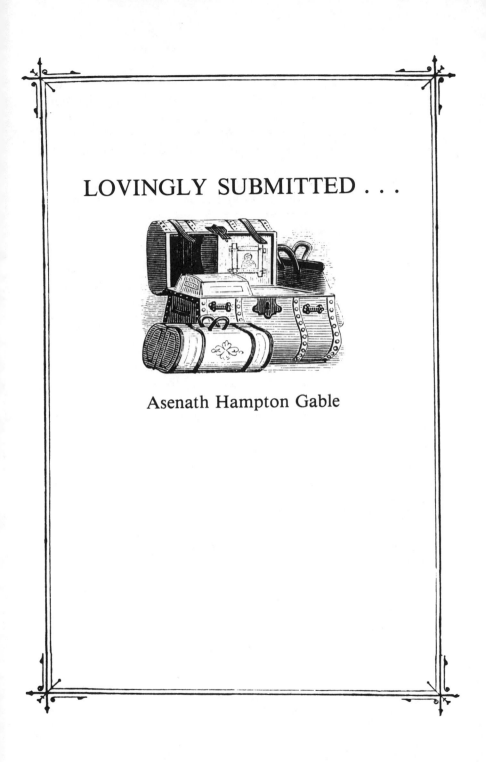

Asenath Hampton Gable

THE ROOTS of most Iowans go "back east." Such was the case of Asenath Hampton, who, motherless at age fifteen, recalled climbing into the wagon, seating herself on a dry goods box, and commencing her journey to the far West. The point of beginning was Ohio. The time was 1855. The final destination was western Iowa.

Asenath was traveling with her brother and the two of them would join their father and other members of the family in eastern Iowa. The trip and her first two years in Iowa were a story in themselves. But those experiences were only a prelude to her marriage, the raising of eleven children, deprivations of a now almost unbelievable nature, loneliness, lack of medical care, unfortunate moves, and at times fearful panic when less-than-friendly Indians roamed the countryside.

Yet Asenath, with courage beyond comprehension and the support of a husband who had "two strong hands that would work for me and a heart that would love and cherish me," took all this with remarkably steady stride, welcomed each new baby with love and affection, and looked forward with seemingly utter faith.

Even more remarkably she had capacity to realize that her story was priceless and worth recording. So at sixty-one, in 1901, she set about to tell what she knew about her own Quaker family origins, her husband's German ancestry, and her own graphic experiences in coming to the "far West." She gave a handwritten copy to each of her ten surviving children.

The excerpts appearing here were chosen by her grand-daughter, Rowena Gable Malone, who has known her only from these pages; she died (July 8, 1907) before many of her grandchildren were born.

Most of the purely personal comments have been deleted, leaving only relevant descriptions of places and events of common interest.

The full history is 126 pages in length, typed from the original text to preserve the faded pages.

I N the spring of 1854 my father's roving disposition asserted itself and he moved to Iowa. [He] kept writing for Brother Solomon and myself to come and live with him. Solomon decided to go and persuaded me to go with him. In the spring of 1855, Solomon got a team and came to Albany for me. We went to Sister Emily's [who] lived twenty miles from Portsmouth on the Ohio River. This was the nearest place where we could get onto a steamboat. Emily's husband kept a store and the goods all had to be hauled from Portsmouth in wagons. We engaged one of these teamsters to carry us to the river.

On April 30, 1855, we bade a tearful adieu to our sister and her husband and started on our journey. The big wagon which we had engaged to carry us to the river had bows on top, over which was stretched white cotton cloth for protection from sun, wind, and rain. Climbing into the wagon, we seated ourselves on a dry goods box and commenced our journey to the West.

My mind was full of romantic thoughts and I looked forward to our journey with pleasant anticipation.

We did not talk much at first. We both realized that we were taking an important step that would change the course of our future lives and each one was occupied with his own thoughts.

We jogged on, over rough, stony roads, over steep hills, and through long stretches of woods which were just beginning to don their spring robes of green velvet. Occasionally we passed a log house with a stick chimney, one door and one window. The man of the house was usually wielding the ax, laying low the monarchs of the forest, or else preparing the few acres of land which had already been cleared for the sowing of seed.

The wife could often be seen at work in the garden, and there were sure to be beds made for the dear old-fashioned flowers. These pioneer sons and daughters of toil possessed fine sentiments, as well as sterling principles of virtue and integrity. We passed a few better houses, with larger clearings surrounding them. But that part of Ohio was thinly populated at that time, and most of the people were very poor. They were hewing out of the forests homes for themselves and their children, and they were happy and contented, a marked contrast to the extravagance of the present day.

At noon we stopped under a poplar tree whose widespreading branches afforded a delightful shade. After eating our lunch and resting for an hour, we again climbed into the wagon and proceeded on our way. We soon came to a maple sugar orchard or camp. It was deserted for sugar-making was past for that year. February and March is the time for making sugar in southern Ohio. It was a large orchard of beautiful maple trees. The wooden troughs which had been used to catch the sweet sap as it ran from the alder spouts which had been driven into holes in the trees were still there in great numbers. Sugar-making was a great event when I was a child. What fun it was to go out to the sugar camp of an evening and watch the fires which were made of great logs of wood and brush, to boil down the sap into sugar.

We rode until nearly sundown when we halted before a log house. The driver went in and asked for a night's lodging for himself and passengers. He wished to stop before entering the city in order to avoid a hotel bill. The early settlers of Ohio were very hospitable and the country folk seldom charged anything for a meal of victuals or a night's lodging.

We were made welcome by the good man and his wife, and we were very glad to get out of the wagon for we were tired and hungry. We greatly enjoyed the supper of ham and eggs, bread and butter, which was soon ready for us.

When bedtime came, I was told to go upstairs and I would find a bed. I mounted the ladder which stood in one corner of the room, and by the light of a lamp which was made of a broken tea saucer, a twisted rag for a wick and coon oil to burn, I discovered a bed on the floor. It was very clean with nicely ironed sheets and pillowcases.

When I blew out my lamp I felt lonely and afraid. Many dangers were presented to my mind, and I wished I had not started on such a journey which I then imagined to be so fraught with danger. Then I remembered my mother's words that God would

ROWENA MALONE

Asenath Hampton Gable was born in Virginia, July 2, 1840. She was an Iowa pioneer, moving to Blackhawk County from Ohio in her fifteenth year. After her marriage in 1856, she and her husband, Solomon Levi, began farming in Iowa, finally locating in Crawford County and retiring to Denison in 1895.

always take care of me if I would put my trust in Him. Rising from my bed, I knelt down and asked the Father to take care of my brother and myself and to guide us safely to the end of our journey. What a blessing is believing prayer. Immediately my fears were all gone and I was soon asleep, and did not awaken until the next morning when I heard our hostess preparing breakfast.

The man we were with kindly drove to the steamboat landing and left us and our boxes on the wharfboat. We had to wait there several hours. We looked at the river rolling by in all its grandeur until we were tired, and then we took a walk through the city. Portsmouth was an old river town without much enterprise, and it presented a very dingy appearance. We returned to the wharfboat about noon, a steamboat soon after landed and Brother Solomon engaged our passage to Cincinnati which was as far down the river as that boat was going. We were soon gliding down the river and in a few hours we arrived at Cincinnati. Here we got onto a large boat which was going to New Orleans and we had to change boats again at Cairo where the Ohio empties into the Mississippi River. There was a steamer waiting at the wharf and we were soon going up the Mississippi on it. At St. Louis we had to make another change. After waiting several hours we got on a boat which carried us to Dubuque, Iowa.

We were fifteen days making the trip. I enjoyed it very much. The weather was fine most of the time, and the scenery along the river was very interesting. We landed in Dubuque in the night. There was no wharfboat there then and the boatmen laid down some planks for us to walk out on, carried our boxes ashore, and left us to our fate. It was very dark. There was no street lamp or anything to show us which way to go. The place was new and there was no plain road leading from the river to the town. It is not strange that I was frightened. We were only children. Solomon was seventeen and I was not quite fifteen years old. We were in a strange place and did not know where to go or what to do. But our mother's God did not forsake her children. He guided us to a place of safety. I clung tremblingly to my brother's arm, and leaving our boxes on the bank of the river we went up to the town to try and find lodging for the rest of the night. This was hard to do. At that time there was a great emigration to the West and the hotels were crowded to their utmost capacity. We finally found a kindhearted landlord who took us in. He gave Solomon a bed on the floor in the barroom, and I slept on the lounge in the dining room. In the morning we had a big bill to pay which reminded us we were no longer in Ohio but in the West where everyone must look after their own interests and where to get the almighty dollar appeared to be the only object in life.

We took the stagecoach for Independence, paying our last cent of money for the fare. It was a very uncomfortable mode of traveling. The road was rough and the coach was crowded with men, women, and children. The women scolded, the babies cried, and the men smoked in sullen silence except when they were asked by the driver to walk uphill which was quite often. Then they would utter exclamations of wrath. I felt like crying with the poor babies but Brother Sol could always see the comic side of everything, and he kept me laughing by his droll remarks.

The horses were changed every 10 or 12 miles so we made good time. If I remember right, we were about 24 hours going from Dubuque to Independence . . . a distance of 75 miles.

When we got to Independence, Sol left me there and walked out to where father lived which was about 7 miles. That afternoon father came after me with a team. I was glad to get to the end of our journey but it did not seem much like home. Father [a physician] lived in a little frame house with only one room, and furnished with the barest necessities. But in this respect they were as well off as their neighbors. There were no railroads then to bring the comforts of life to the door of the settlers. Everything had to be hauled from the Mississippi River with teams.

We stayed with father a few days and then went 20 miles across the prairie to visit Sister Mary Ellis and Brother Hiram Hampton. They had moved to Iowa several years previous to this and each one had secured a good farm and were in prosperous circumstances. Sister Mary and husband were anxious to have me make my home with them. They had no children of their own and Sister Mary had promised our mother to care for us younger children. This promise she faithfully kept so far as it was possible for her to do.

Father wanted me to live with him, but he was not able to provide for me. The inhabitants where he lived were few in number and were remarkably healthy, a few cases of ague being about all the sickness there was. Therefore there was but little for a physician to do. Father never had anything laid up for future use and he was at that time in very embarrassing circumstances. But with his usual want of discretion, he insisted on my living with them, and after I had visited with brother and sister a few days, he sent for me to come home and I stayed with them until they

Some "went West" by covered wagon. But many—among them Asenath Hampton—came down the Ohio by steamboat. Asenath, age fifteen, began her journey in 1855. This type of steamboat (this is the *Pargoud* docked at St. Louis) was operating from about that time until 1870.

moved back east and then I went to Sister Mary Ellis and lived with her as one of the family.

COURTSHIP AND MARRIAGE

I was fifteen years old when I went to live with Sister Mary. My sister and brother being older and I being old for my age, and very large (I did not grow any in height after I was twelve) I went into society with them when I was quite young. I had seen a good

11

deal of the world for one of my age. I had been in several different families and had observed that there were many unhappy homes. Among the women, more than the men, were many who had married in haste to repent at leisure. I think there were more unhappy marriages formerly than at the present time. The world is growing wiser and better. Girls do not marry as young as they used to, and are better able to choose congenial companions. Sister Emily married at the age of eighteen. She had a loving husband with good business ability and they lived happily together, but her health was delicate after her marriage and she was confined to the house most of the time. Her life appeared to me to be very dull and uninteresting compared to the free, easy life she had lived before her marriage. I thought of all this and came to the conclusion that I would keep clear of matrimony. I decided that I would enjoy life while young. I would live with Sister Mary until Brother Solomon was settled in life and then live with him. I was sure that he would share his prosperity with me. I expected him to marry and have a nice home, and I would picture myself as occupying an honorary place in his family. I would be a dignified old maid, but I would keep my heart young and affectionate and be always ready to give sympathy and encouragement to all who were in need of help. In this way, I expected to win the love and respect of all my friends. This was one of my air castles and it was very different from what I have found the realities of life to be. But now when old age is upon me I can look back over my past life and recognize the guiding hand of Providence that has safely led me thus far. Sometimes the way seemed rough and hedged with thorns. "Into each life some rain must fall." We need lessons of adversity to wean our affections from this world and to teach us to lay up treasures in heaven. I have had my trials but my blessings have been far more numerous. My husband is an honorable man, and is devoted to me, and no mother ever had more loving children than mine have always been to me, and I would not exchange the wealth of my family's affection for any worldly possession or fame.

But I am getting ahead of my story. When I went to live with Sister Mary, there was a young man named Solomon Levi Gable working on the farm for them. In those days, there was no social distinction between the employed and the employers on the farm and I was introduced to him. I took no further notice of him at first, and he appeared to ignore my presence altogether. I had been accustomed to having some little attention paid to me by any gentleman friends and his apparent indifference piqued me and I determined that if he did not want to be sociable I would show him that it made no difference to me. Several weeks passed without our speaking to each other after our introduction. After awhile I became interested in this silent man, although I tried not to notice him. Sometimes our eyes would meet and then greatly to my mortification I would feel the blood rush to my face. Indeed, I think we were both hopelessly in love before a word was spoken after our introduction. What a strange thing conjugal love is. Every person feels it sometime in life but who can explain it? I doubt if the genuine article ever comes to the same person more than once in a lifetime.

I began to feel that this man's presence was necessary to my happiness but I could not understand why it was so. I was afraid that he would notice my interest in him; this made me shy and bashful in his presence. After several weeks he made some casual remark to me and I answered. Sister Mary had noticed our reserved manner toward each other and she laughingly remarked that the ice was broken between us. Soon after this he presented a ring to me. I hesitated about accepting it for I had been taught that it was not proper to accept presents from gentlemen. But he appeared so hurt at my refusal that I accepted and wore it. After this, by mutual, unspoken consent we were lovers. My former resolutions about matrimony were all gone and in their place an undying love which took entire possession of me. My romantic imagination invested my lover with all that was noble, generous, and good. The thought that he loved me and that I was necessary to his happiness filled me with delight. We were both poor in worldly goods but I cared nothing for that. He told me that he had two strong hands that would work for me and a heart that would ever love and cherish me. He assured me that we would soon have a little home of our own where we would live in the enjoyment of peace, love, and happiness.

One year passed, a happy, blissful year. How often in after-years when the burdens of life seemed greater than I could bear have I looked back to that joyful, never-to-be-forgotten year of our courtship.

We were married at the home of Sister Mary Ellis near Waterloo, Iowa, on June 12, 1856.

HOUSEKEEPING

At the time of our marriage, my husband had George Ellis's farm rented. We boarded with them until fall and then we went to housekeeping in their old house. It was built of logs with one door and one window and a large fireplace in one end of the room.

Our furniture consisted of a bedstead, three chairs, a table, and secondhand cook stove. We set up the stove in the opposite end of the cabin from the fireplace. There were some shelves on one side of the room, made by boring holes in the logs, driving wooden pins into them, and then laying rough boards on the pins. I covered the boards with newspapers which I scalloped very artistically and then arranged my dishes, which Sister Mary had given me, on them. I spread out the dishes so as to show off to good advantage. My bed was covered with a quilt which I was very proud of. The blocks were made of red, green, and yellow calico, and set together with white muslin. I had pieced it before I was married and Sister Mary had helped me quilt it.

I hung a white curtain around the bottom of the bedstead and this made a convenient place to stow away things which I wished to keep out of sight.

A breadth of white muslin made a curtain for the window, which I looped back and tied with faded ribbon.

When I had everything arranged I surveyed my domicile with as much satisfaction as a queen might her palace. We commenced housekeeping in November, 1856. The following winter was the coldest ever known in Iowa. It was no uncommon thing that winter for the thermometer to register 40 below zero and blizzards were of frequent occurrence. Many persons froze to death in the northern part of this state and other places in the West.

We had some experience with blizzards that winter. At one time we went to Waterloo (5 miles from where we lived) to spend the day with Cousin James Hampton and wife. It was pleasant in the morning when we started, but in the afternoon it commenced to snow and we started home early. We had not gone far before the wind began to blow fearfully. The clouds of snow shut out the light of day, and we could not see the road. The sudden darkness, the deafening roar of the wind, and the intense cold made up an experience which is not easily forgotten. As my husband could not see the road, he gave the lines to the horses, trusting to their instinct to take us home. The snow had been packed and graded up in the road by the constant travel on the snow since it had blown on the road until it was several feet deep. If the horses left the beaten track, they could not travel, for the snowdrifts in many places were 8 and 10 feet deep and we would certainly have perished for it was so cold it was all that we could do to keep from

When Asenath Hampton Gable married, she and her husband began housekeeping near Waterloo in a house that "was built of logs with one door and one window and a large fireplace in one end of the room." (1838)

freezing as it was. But the faithful horses kept the road and carried us safely home.

For six weeks that winter it did not thaw enough to moisten the snow on the south side of the roofs of houses. A great many people had settled in the Northwest the previous summer and were not prepared to encounter such a winter. Much of their stock died for want of food and shelter and many of the people's resources were exhausted when the long winter came to an end. But we were very comfortable between two fires in our little cabin. It was so cold and the snow was so deep that my husband could do nothing more than the chores, get wood, and keep the two fires burning day and night.

There was very little game there at that time and the weather was too bad to hunt much. Brother Solomon stayed with George and Mary Ellis that winter and sometimes George, Sol, and Levi would go out for a short time in the middle of the day to hunt. They would have lots of sport for Brother Solomon could make sport out of almost anything. They used to say that Sol scared the rabbits so with his shouts and laughter that they could not run.

I was busy with my housework and sewing and spent much of my time in fancywork and embroidery. The long evenings we spent in reading such books and papers as we could get, and in playing innocent games. Thus the long cold winter passed pleasantly away.

MOVING AND VISITING

In the spring of 1857, we moved from Blackhawk County to Van Buren County, Iowa. My husband's sister Eliza lived there and his mother lived near there in Davis County. We owned a good team of horses and a wagon which we covered in immigrant fashion, and putting into the wagon our household goods, we bade adieu to Sister Mary and husband and started to move. It was May 27, 1857, but the snowdrifts of the previous hard winter were not all gone from the north hillsides. We had a very disagreeable journey. The weather was unpleasant and the roads bad. Sometimes the wagon would get stuck in the mud, and we would have to get another team to help pull it out.

Our baby was only seven weeks old when we started to move and riding all day in the wagon was hard on him. He would sometimes cry until late at night. This made us realize the truth of the adage, "There is no rose without a thorn."

When we came to the Des Moines River it was very high, and looked frightful to me. There was no way to cross but to ford it. I thought we would surely be drowned if we attempted to drive across. It was almost dark which made it appear more dangerous. We saw a man on the other side of the river and my husband called to him and asked if we could cross. The man said we could if we would drive into the river, then go upstream to a certain point, then drive down to the landing, thus avoiding a deep hole in the middle of the stream. The bottom of the river was rough with large stones, the water so muddy we could not see the stones to avoid them. I think I was never more frightened in my life. I held my baby tightly in my arms expecting every moment the wagon would upset and we would be at the mercy of the dark waters. But we had a good team and my husband was a skillful driver and we went over in safety. We drove 5 miles further that night to the home of my husband's sister Eliza. She and her husband gave us a warm reception. I was very thankful to get to the end of our journey. We had been five days on the road and baby and I were very tired.

We visited there a few days and then went to see my husband's mother. We found her very comfortable, living on a farm surrounded with plenty. My mother-in-law was delighted to see us, and tried to make it pleasant for us and to make me feel at home, but I stood somewhat in awe of her and never became very familiar.

After visiting with my husband's mother for a few days, we went back to his sister's and moved into a house belonging to them and he went to work for his brother-in-law, but did not work long on account of poor health. It was a very unhealthy place, on the river bottom in the timber. My husband was unable to work all summer, and I was not very well, had to take quinine much of the time to keep from having the ague. In the fall I had the bilious fever and had to have a physician called. This was a dark time for us. Sunshine and shadow mingle together. We had been on expenses all summer and were not earning anything. The little money whch we had saved was nearly all gone. My former air castles were tottering on their foundations and our prospects looked very gloomy. The "darkest hour is just before the day." About this time Brother George Ellis came to see us. He had sold his farm in Blackhawk County and was looking for another location. We were very dissatisfied with the place where we were then living and therefore my husband took his team and went with George Ellis to try and find a better location. The wagon was covered and they went prepared to camp out. That trip did my husband more good than any medicine could have done. He was hardly able to walk when he started. He began to improve immediately. They were gone about three weeks. When he returned, he was well and strong. He brought back a load of apples from Missouri and sold part of them to pay the expenses of the trip. He did not find a place that suited him to move to.

Soon after this he got employment and went to work with renewed energy. My health also improved as the weather got cooler. Our star of hope again shone brightly. My husband worked all winter and earned enough to buy a cow and provisions to last nearly all of the next summer.

Our brother-in-law Vincent Cheadle and family had moved to Crawford County, Iowa, the year before and they kept writing for us to come where they were. After considering the matter for some time we decided to go to them. On April 1, 1858, after bidding our relatives adieu we again loaded our possessions into the wagon, tied our cow to the end of it, and started for Crawford County where we have made our home ever since. My husband's brother Uriah accompanied us. Our last day's drive was the hardest one we had while making the move. We stopped all night at a place called Brushey Ford in Carroll County. We started early in the morning hoping to get to Mr. Cheadle's that day. We travelled 30 miles without seeing any sign of human habitation. We halted about noon by a stream of water, fed our team, ate a cold lunch, and then started again on our weary way. It had been cloudy and disagreeable all day and about the middle of the afternoon it began to rain. This made the roads slippery and we had to drive slow. We were tired but there was no place to stop for shelter and we had to go on. It was dark when we got to Mason's Grove. We were not acquainted with the road which led us up steep hills and down into deep hollows. It was so dark we could not see the road, and my husband had to walk before the horses to prevent them from going against a tree or into a ditch.

It seemed to me as we went over the steep-sided places that the wagon would upset and we would be killed. The long ride, the rain, and darkness had unnerved me, and I sat in the wagon trembling with fear, holding Byron in my arms. I did not speak of my fears to the others. They had trials enough of their own. Uriah was walking behind the wagon to attend to the cow and Levi went before to lead the horses. We were all wet, tired, hungry, and almost discouraged when we saw the light of a tallow candle shining from a cabin window. This was a cheering sight to us. We soon came to the house and were kindly received by the inmates. The rain was pouring down, and the lightning and thunder were terrific, but we were soon sheltered from their fury. Our poor, faithful horses had to stand out in the storm all night.

The good housewife soon had supper ready for us. It consisted of hot coffee, biscuits, and fried bacon of which we partook with good appetites and thankful hearts.

After supper we made a bed on the floor and were soon asleep. But all night in my dreams I was riding down hills and crossing deep hollows.

The next morning we were somewhat refreshed. Our troubles of the previous day were over and we could laugh about our fears.

Mr. Cheadle lived about a mile from where we had stopped for the night. After breakfast we drove over to their house and were warmly welcomed by them. After resting and visiting a short time my husband started out to find a place to live. We soon succeeded in renting a farm of 40 acres and we went to housekeeping again.

OUR FIRST SUMMER IN CRAWFORD COUNTY, IOWA

The house was pleasantly situated on a hill with a fine view of the surrounding country. We could see Mason's Grove, and the Boyer River valley for miles. The house was a little frame building not more than 12 by 14 feet. After the weather got warm the owner put up a little shed at one end of the house for my cook stove. This was a great comfort to me. The house had a nice, smooth floor in it. This was a luxury which I had not enjoyed before since I began housekeeping, and I took great pride in keeping it nice and white. I had never heard of a painted floor at that time and a carpet was far beyond my highest ambition. I was therefore very happy scrubbing the floor of our little shanty. I had a supply of flower seed which my mother-in-law had given me. I soon had a nice flower bed made. I planted morning glories at the windows and in a short time I had window curtains which for beauty rivalled the richest lace. It was a solitary place, there was no road by it, and no neighbors near. But we were too busy to get very lonely.

After we got settled we had six dollars in money and my husband spent that for seed wheat. We did not have any more money for six months and but very little for several years. There appeared to be no money in the country. People talk about hard times now, but they know nothing about getting along as we did then. A man could not get a day's work, and if he had anything to sell there was no money to buy it.

We brought a supply of provisions when we came there. We had smoked ham, flour, dried fruit, and groceries. We had a cow which furnished us with milk and butter, so we lived well for a time, but after a few months our supplies became exhausted and we had no money to replenish our larder. Therefore we had to do without everything but the barest necessities of life. We made a substitute for coffee of corn. I would roast it, grind it in the coffee mill, and try and make believe that it was good coffee. When the flour gave out we had to resort to cornmeal. The year before we came here the corn was badly injured by early frosts and it was soft and hardly fit for food. My husband got some corn from Mr. Cheadle and paid for it in work. He picked out the best of it for bread. The rest he fed to the horses. There was a saw mill on Boyer River and the owner, to accommodate settlers, put in a set of stones to grind corn. They were 8 inches across and capable of grinding about 2 bushels of corn a day. Of course the miller had to take a good share of the corn for grinding it. Our cow went dry the latter part of the summer and we had to do without milk and butter, mix our cornbread with water, and drink our corn coffee without cream or sugar. After the meat which we brought with us was gone, I did not have grease enough about the house to grease the bread pans and the cornbread would stick fast to the pans. Game was scarce here at that time, nearly all the deer perished during the hard winter of 1856–1857. The snow was very deep and a hard crust formed on top of it. Men and dogs could walk on the crusted snow, but the deer would break through when they ran and thus became easy prey for the hunter. The few that survived the winter went south in the spring. It was two or three years after before a deer was seen here. A few came in then, but they were never very plentiful after the hard winter. There were a few prairie chickens and squirrels. My husband sometimes shot one, but he did not have much time to hunt during the summer and ammunition was scarce. We raised a good garden and had plenty of vegetables. They were a little dry without any meat or butter but we had good appetites and managed to live quite comfortably. We never suffered for want of food. Our little boy soon tired of the cornbread and would not eat it, but we raised some fine squashes which he liked and he lived principally on them. He was healthy and happy and a great comfort to us.

The wheat for which we had paid our last six dollars was nearly a failure. My husband cut it with a scythe and threshed it with a flail. This threshing machine was made by tying two sticks together. One stick was used as a handle and the other to beat out the grain. After it was threshed it had to be separated from the chaff. This was done by pouring it from one vessel to another (he used my dishpan and washtub for this) and letting the wind blow the chaff away. After it was threshed and cleaned we had about one bushel of wheat. Of course this had to be ground into flour before we could have any wheat bread.

Some enterprising yankee had erected a steam mill near Denison. My husband took his crop of wheat to this mill to get it ground. When he got there he found the fire was out and the establishment without fuel. The miller told him that he would have to draw them a load of wood before they could grind his wheat. He had to submit to this demand and he drove to the timber about a mile distant and procured a load of wood. He helped the miller make a fire and get up steam. Then he waited for his grist to be ground. After the miller had tolled it there was about 15 or 20 pounds of flour left for us, and that was all the flour we had until the next fall.

We raised sugar cane that summer but we had no way to make it into syrup until my husband and Mr. Cheadle put their inventive skill together and constructed a cane mill. It was a crude machine for they had but few tools to work with, but it mashed the cane, and pressed out the juice and we made some very good molasses which was a very acceptable addition to our bill of fare.

When we first came here in 1858, there was an M. E. [Methodist] church and S. S. [Sunday school] established in Mason's Grove. There was but one M. E. Conference in northern Iowa at that time. The man that was to come here lived in the eastern part of the state. He had to be moved to this county in a wagon. We had a good span of horses and my husband was asked to move the preacher. As he was out of employment (the corn was not ready to gather) and greatly in need of money, he consented to do so. He thought it would take him about two weeks to make the trip. It began to rain soon after he started and continued to rain nearly all the time that he was gone. This made the roads bad and the streams (nearly all of which had to be forded as there were but few bridges in northern Iowa at that time) were so high that he had to go around the head of some of them to get across. Some days after traveling all day he would be only a little nearer home at night than he was in the morning. Instead of two weeks as he had expected, it was thirty-one days before he returned home. It was a hard trip for him. His clothing was wet for days at a time. When they stopped for the night it would be in a little shanty with only a cook stove to warm by. Of course the minister's wife and babies (they had two little children) had to have the warm corner and there was no chance for the men to dry their garments. Nearly every day they would get sloughed down . . . that is, the horses and wagon would break through the sod and sink so deep in the mire they could not get out until the wagon was unloaded. The men had to carry the preacher's wife and children and the household goods out to where the ground was solid. Then they tied a rope to the end of the wagon tongue, hitched the horses to it, and drew the wagon out of the slough. They would then load in the goods and the wife and babies and go until they came to another slough when the same thing had to be gone through with again.

When they came to the Coon River it was too high to ford, and there was no way to cross except on a new bridge which did not have the floor laid. My husband procured some planks and laid them lengthwise across from one timber to another. He then led the horses over one at a time on the single plank. The horses had been through so many hard places they had become very docile and would try to do anything that he told them to do. After they got the horses over, they carried over the goods. Then they tied the long rope to the wagon and towed it across the river.

Before my husband went to move the preacher, he engaged Mr. Cheadle's oldest boy who was then about twelve years old to stay with me for company and do the chores. But in two or three days after he started, Mr. Cheadle was taken sick with typhoid fever and his boy had to go home. This left me alone with Byron. He was only eighteen months old, but he was lots of company and a great comfort to me. I tried to make the best of the situation. I kept busy with my housework and sewing. The first two weeks passed quickly. Then I began to long for his return. The weather was bad. It rained nearly all the time. This made it more lonely for me. The sun did not shine for days at a time. I did not hear from my husband while he was away. I became more and more anxious about him. Sometimes I imagined that he had been robbed and murdered by horse thieves. He drove a very valuable team and as there were a great many desperate characters throughout the country, I feared they had killed him for his team. Then I would think about the high water I knew he had to cross. The continued rain would make the streams everywhere more dangerous. I became too anxious to work my embroidery. It was laid aside and I would sit by the window with folded hands, watching for his return while the weary hours dragged slowly by. Young as he was, Byron seemed to understand my feelings. He was very quiet and would often leave his play and climb into my lap, put his little arms around my neck and kiss me. I do not know how I could have endured the suspense if it had not been for my little boy's sympathy. At last one evening about dark, my husband returned and there was great rejoicing in our little home. We forgot our past fears and trials in the joy of again being united.

He was very tired and the horses which we both thought so much of looked as if they were ruined. But they were young and hardy and with good care soon recovered. The money we had hoped to get and for which we had suffered so much we never received. The preacher, like most Methodist preachers of that time, was not burdened with money. The people he came to serve had all they could do to pay him enough to live on after he got here, without paying his traveling expenses. But he was a good man and did good service for the Master here and no doubt will have his reward.

After my husband returned we went to work with renewed courage. The corn was ready to husk and was a good crop which was encouraging. We could not sell it for there was no market here, but we knew if we had plenty of corn, we could live. After a time, we had a chance to trade corn for a cow and two pigs. Our prospects began to brighten. The weather, too, which had been bad for so long cleared up. The sun shone out in all its glory. We lived on a hill and had splendid views of the grand sunrises and sunsets. We could also see Mason's Grove in its gorgeous array of crimson and gold. There was another great sight which we enjoyed very much during this summer of 1858—it was the most brilliant comet I have ever seen. It was visible every evening for several weeks. Some people though it was a bad omen, that some great calamity was about to come upon us, or that it would come in contact with the earth and crush it out of existence. But I only thought of its beauty, the great immensity of space through which it was wanderer, and of its Great Creator. It is true that the great Civil War soon followed after the appearance of this comet. But I do not think it had any connection with it.

Game was still scarce but in the fall a few wild ducks and geese would stop along the river. One day my husband shot two fine ducks. They fell on the opposite side of the river, and he had to go downstream about a mile to cross on the bridge. When he got around to where the ducks had fallen he found that an eagle had preceded him and had eaten so much of his ducks it could not fly. He caught it and led it home by the wing. It was a fine specimen of that emblematic bird, and it made a brave fight for its life. When he got the eagle home he thought he would try the courage of a hound dog which was a great favorite. The dog was afraid of the huge bird and would not attack it. Then my husband threw it on him. The eagle immediately caught the dog and fastened its talons on his throat and choked him and he could not breathe. My husband tried to unfasten its grip on the dog, but finding he could not do so, he called to his brother Uriah to help him. Their combined efforts were not sufficient to free the dog and in order to save the dog's life, they cut off the leg of the eagle.

The first winter we spent in this county was passed very pleasantly. We had become accustomed to our primitive mode of living. Good health enabled us to enjoy our plain food, and our little boy was a constant source of pleasure to us. What few books we had were read over again. I had several volumes of a magazine *The Ladies Repository.* It was published by the Methodist Book Concern and was an excellent periodical. Sister Mary had subscribed for it for me before I was married and I had preserved the numbers. After we came out here I read and reread them so often I still remember many of the articles although over forty years have passed since then. One poem titled "Soul Life," I committed to memory and I can still repeat it. I do not know who the author was but it has been to me one of the most helpful poems I have ever read. When life's burdens have been hard to bear, I have often recalled its beautiful language and lofty sentiment and have thereby been encouraged to go forward and cheerfully discharge the homely duties of life.

RENTING ANOTHER FARM

In the spring of 1859, we rented a farm near Denison. As there was no house on it, we rented one in the town of Denison which at that time had only a few houses in it. It was a wet, late spring. We moved on April 19. There was still snow on the ground. The day we moved was very disagreeable. We had two children [Byron and Ida Alice] and I had my hands full. The eldest was but two years and our girl baby one month old. We had to ride in the big wagon which was loaded with our household goods. It was a 9 mile drive, the roads were bad and we had to drive slowly. Before we got to Denison, the baby began to cry and I felt very much like doing the same. I knew the house we were going into would be cold. Our stove was in the wagon and it would take a long time to get it set up and the house warmed. But a pleasant surprise awaited us. What a blessing is kindness. How it dispells our gloomy thoughts and causes life to take on a brighter aspect. A dear, good family named Comfort (they were comforters to us) lived next door to the house we were going into. They invited us into their home and gave us a good, warm dinner. Then Mr. Comfort helped my husband set up the stove. After the house got warm, I heartily thanked our new friends for their kindness and then went over to inspect the house which was to be our home for some time to come. It was quite a good house for those days. It had plenty of room for our small amount of furniture.

We both found that now we had plenty of work to do. It was late in the season to begin farming. My husband had to go about one mile to his work and he had to plow the ground before he could sow the wheat and oats. He found when he began to plow the land that it had been misrepresented to him. The man he rented it from, told him it had been broken up in good season the year before, but the truth was that it had not been broken until late in the fall and the sod had not rotted. This made the ground in bad condition. But there was no help for it then, and he had to do the best he could. It was hard work and poor pay that year. It was so late before he got the small grain sowed it did not amount to much. He worked very hard to raise a good crop of corn but in this he was also disappointed. There came a frost in August which killed the corn before any of it was ripe. He had sowed some buckwheat in the spring and it was just in blossom when the frost came and killed it. This caused our visions of buckwheat cakes for the next winter to vanish.

I, too, had my trials that summer as well as my husband. I found it very hard work taking care of two babies and doing my housework. Byron kept me constantly watching him. He was not content in the house and when I let him out he would run away and I would have to hunt him. One day he went to the town well, climbed into the watering trough, and when I found him he was dipping up water with his little straw hat and shouting "hurrah!" as he swung it over his head. We had just been to a Fourth of July celebration where he had heard the people cheering and he was celebrating by adding cheers and water together.

We had to carry all the water a long distance, and as my husband had to go so far to his work, and had so much to do, I carried most of it. My washings were quite large, as I had two little children to wash for and it took a good deal of water. We had two cows and I made butter to sell. I also took in some plain sewing to get some things which we needed badly. Altogether it was too much for my strength and my health began to fail. I lost my appetite, grew thin and weak. I could not get my work done and after a few weeks had to keep to my bed. Fortunately for us, there was a physician here at that time who had been called from a distance to treat a lady of Denison. (There was no physician living in this county at that time.) My husband called that physician and he gave me some medicine that broke up the fever and I soon recovered. We lived in Denison one year and then moved to Coon Grove, 4 miles south of Denison. The farm we rented there was a good one and we raised good crops. The house was an old-fashioned log cabin very much like the one we lived in when we first went to keeping house. It was a very secluded place in a natural grove of timber. I enjoyed the scenery very much. A beautiful little stream of water meandered through the grove. There were a great many wild flowers, and numerous birds furnished us with excellent music free of charge. We seldom went to church while we lived there. Our horses as well as ourselves were too tired to go so far on Sunday. There was no place of worship nearer than Denison. I would often take the children out in the grove on Sunday afternoon and enjoy the fresh air, birds, flowers, and trees.

We had but few neighbors, and seldom had any company. There was one family living about a mile from us whom we sometimes visited. I remember the first time I went there I was much pleased with the dinner. They did not have a cook stove and did their cooking by the fireplace. There was an iron rod across the chimney with hooks attached to it to hang the kettles on. The iron teakettle and the pot to boil the potatoes in were hung over the fire. Then some of the live coals were shoveled out on the stone hearth to sit the frying pan on in which to fry the ham and eggs. On another pile of coals was a large flatiron pan to bake the corn cakes on. The coffee pot had its place on the hearth. I think the coffee was made of browned corn.

One of the daughters set the table while the hostess attended to the cooking. In a very short time (much sooner than it could have been done on a cook stove) a bountiful dinner was on the table. Everything was very neat. The cloth was a coarse cotton one, but it was spotless and nicely ironed.

My husband raised good crops while we were in Coon Grove but there was no market for his grain. We had a good many hogs and in the winter he butchered a wagonload and hauled them to Sioux City, a distance of nearly 90 miles. After he got them there he only got $2.50 per hundred. When the expenses were paid, there was not much left, but we had learned to get along with very little money and also that it did no good to complain.

We raised enough wheat for bread, but it caused us a great deal of labor before it was ready for the table. The threshing machine was somewhat an improvement over the flail before mentioned but was still a very crude affair. It did not separate the chaff so that had to be done by a fanning mill turned by hand.

I had to cook for several men for a week, while they threshed out 50 bushels of wheat. Then after it was cleaned up it had to be hauled 50 miles to mill. The steam mill before mentioned had been abandoned for want of patronage as there was very little wheat raised here at that time. We raised our own meat, pork, beef, and chickens, an abundance of vegetables, with plenty of milk, butter, and honey. So we had plenty to eat that was good enough for anybody. But how to get clothes was a serious matter. We had brought a good supply of clothing here with us, but I had been obliged to make over some of my dresses for the children, and my husband had worn his clothes until they were threadbare, and I was tired of mending them. We all needed shoes. I made moccasins for the children out of skins of wild animals which their father tanned, but they were not very nice, and I always wanted to see our children look pretty.

Fortunately my husband knew how to trap fur-bearing animals. He had brought some traps here with him and as soon as the weather got cold, he was busy hunting and trapping. He caught some splendid specimens. Some of the mink and otter had such fine, glossy fur that it would glisten in the sunlight like changeable silk. He caught one beaver that weighed over 60 pounds. He also caught muskrats, wolves, and wildcats.

Fur was in great demand in the East and men came out here to buy it and he found ready sale for all that he could catch. This was a great help to us. It was nearly the only thing that we could get money for and it furnished us with clothing and groceries.

[*Only one record of Asenath Hampton's children is given here, although her history contained records of all. This account of her second son tells of the difficulties of child care and the costs of education*].

GEORGE HARVEY

On November 11, 1860, another child was given to us, a bright little boy, George Harvey. He was a delicate baby and when he was five months old he took a severe cold which developed into lung fever. He was very ill for a long time. As there was no physician in reach of us, I had to depend upon my own resources. I treated him with simple remedies which I had learned to use and nursed him carefully. He got better but was not very well for a long time. He was very fretful and required nearly all of my time to take care of him. All fancywork had to be given up and I could find but little time for reading. There were five of us in the family now. I had to do all the knitting and sewing by hand. We could not buy stockings and ready-made clothing then as we do now. I could not get time to do my sewing in the daytime, for I would not neglect my baby, and he would not go to sleep in the evening until I went to bed with him. Then he would sleep until morning. I would go to bed with him early in the evening, and then get up at three o'clock in the morning. I would stir up the fire in the big fireplace, throw on some wood (my husband always brought in plenty of wood in the evening), light my tallow candle, and then sew or knit until daylight. In this way I did nearly all my sewing and knitting that winter. After George was one year old, his health was better [but] he had a troublesome cough every winter and sometimes would have the asthma, until he was about sixteen years old. Then he had the measles. He was very sick at the time, but when he got over them he was stronger than he had ever been, and he never had the asthma afterward. But he was still troubled with a cough during cold weather. We sent him to school when he was able to go until he was about ten years old. After that he had to help with the work on the farm in the summer, only going to school three or four months in winter and he often had to stay at home for days on account of his cough. I had so much to claim my attention that I could not give him any assistance with his studies. It looked like a poor prospect for him to get an education but where there is a will there is a way is a very true proverb in many instances.

When he was about sixteen years of age he was converted and joined the M. E. Church. After this he determined to get an education and he overcame every obstacle by patient and untiring perseverance. He scarcely ever read a story or any work of fiction or poetry, but applied himself diligently to his schoolbooks. When he came in the house from work in the field, if the meal was not quite ready, he would improve the few moments by studying. And in the evening when the rest of the family were talking, playing games, or reading a story, George would be working over some difficult problem in arithmetic, or learning a lesson in grammar or geography.

The winter after he was twenty-one, he attended school in Vail, a distance of 4½ miles from home. The snow was deep and sometimes he could hardly get through the snowdrifts, but he would not give up. He walked to school all that winter and made rapid progress in his studies. He would sit up until ten and eleven o'clock at night to get his lessons and then get up in the morning early enough to help with the chores and then walk 4½ miles to school. The next fall after working on the farm all summer, he succeeded in getting a certificate to teach school. He taught the following winter and the next summer he worked by the month for his father. After the corn was gathered at home, he went out to work for the neighbors. He picked corn by the bushel, and by working early and late he made good wages. He would not stop for cold weather and sometimes he picked corn when it was 20 below zero. He saved his money and on the first of January, 1882, he went to Mount Vernon, Iowa, to attend school. Just before he went away to school he was pleasantly surprised by his Uncle George Ellis giving him a gold watch for a namesake present.

At school he continued in the same virtuous way of perseverance, industry, and economy which he had practiced at home. He applied himself diligently to his studies, and stood high in the estimation of his teachers and schoolmates. He stayed in school at Mount Vernon four years, paying his own expenses by working during vacations in the harvest fields, selling books, and doing whatever he could get to do to earn an honest dollar. He made enough with what he had saved up from his earnings before he started to school to take him through.

While George was going to school at Mount Vernon, the Union Publishing House of Chicago offered a good gold watch as a premium to the student of Cornell College at Mount Vernon who would sell the greatest number of books in one week during the summer vacation. A great many of the students tried to get the prize. George came home to canvass among his friends and acquaintances and many of them subscribed for the book because they wanted him to get the prize. I think it was eighty books that he sold in one week. He got the prize which proved to be a valuable watch and also made a big profit on the books that he sold.

After going to Cornell four years, he determined to go to Ann Arbor, Michigan, and take a law course. He graduated from there in 1888. Then he came home and went into the cornfield and working there he got money enough to start in his profession. He then located in Council Bluffs, Iowa, and has lived there ever since.

BUYING A FARM

In the fall of 1860, my husband's sister Susan and husband made us a visit. They had some time before rented their farm in this county and moved to Onawa, a town on the Missouri River. Now they wanted to sell their farm to us. I was tired of renting and having to move so often, and I wanted to have a home of our own. Therefore I was very glad when my husband concluded to buy their farm. It consisted of 80 acres of land, and 30 were under cultivation.

Mr. Cheadle had commenced to build a good-sized frame house on it but he had not finished it. There was only one small room that had been plastered and we had to live in that during the winter. We bought the farm on time and were to pay $750 for it, Mr. Cheadle agreeing to take stock in payment. We had a number of cattle and as they were a good price, we hoped to soon be able to pay for the farm. This was about the beginning of the Civil War. We were too far from a railroad to receive any benefit from the rise in farm produce which the war caused in the eastern part of the country.

Money was still scarce here and the first year of the war, cattle depreciated so much in value that by the time we were ready to move on the farm it looked like it would be much harder to pay for it than when we contracted for it. My husband wanted to give it up after he had made one payment of $150 but Mr. Cheadle would not take it back. He said he would not live here if they would give him all of the county, but said he would take $150 less for the place than had been agreed upon and would not charge us any interest. This encouraged us somewhat and we determined to keep the place and do our best to pay for it.

The farm was rented when we bought it and we could not go on it for one year. Everything looked very discouraging here at that time. The war cloud hung threateningly over our whole country. Rumors of Indian war caused great alarm in the West, and many people began to prepare to leave here for some place of greater safety.

I was not much afraid of the Indians at that time. Still, when

I was alone with our little children I often thought about them and wondered what I would do if they should come. We lived in a lonely place, one mile from a neighbor. It seems strange now that I was not more afraid for I am naturally timid, but I was busy with my housework and taking care of the children and did not have much time to think about Indians.

I remember one time I was badly frightened. Our dog which did not usually bark much at anyone began to bark furiously. I looked out and saw a man coming toward the house. He was dressed in very ragged clothes and had moccasins on his feet. I was afraid he had been with the Indians and that there might be some of them hiding in the woods nearby. The dog disliked the looks of the man as much as I did. This made me more afraid but he did not prove to be dangerous. He came in and asked for something to eat. I gave him some food which he ate, and then he left without a word. I was much more thankful to be rid of him than he appeared to be for his dinner.

Not long after this my husband was sent for to go after some Indians who had stolen horses from a man living near Beloit. A party of men had followed the thieves and overtaken them. They showed fight, and our men fearing they were not strong enough to capture them came back for reinforcements. My husband and about thirty other men went to try and recover the stolen horses, but the thieves had got so far away that they could not overtake them unless they followed them into their own territory and it was thought to be too dangerous to do that and they gave up the chase and came home.

In the fall of 1861 we were joyfully surprised by a number of my relatives coming to make us a visit. Sister Mary Ellis and husband and adopted daughter, Brother Levi Hampton and wife, and Brother Solomon (that was before he was married). There was no railroad here then and they came from the eastern part of the state with a team and wagon. They had a tent and were prepared to camp out. They carried their bedding, cooking utensils, and guns with them. Prairie chickens and other small game were plentiful and they had an abundance of delicious fries.

They were a jolly company. The severe afflictions and sad disappointments of later years had not then dampened our spirits. Laughter, song, and repartee were freely indulged in. The men folks went hunting during the day, and came home at night loaded with game and hungry enough to enjoy the bountiful supper which we women had prepared for them. The evenings were cool and after supper we would build a fire in the big fireplace, gather around the hearthstone, and talk over old times and enjoy each other's company.

The time for parting came all too soon, and we bade our brothers and sisters a tearful adieu.

Their visit was a great blessing to us, not only while they were with us but the memory of it cheered and brightened many an otherwise lonely hour for a long time afterward, and even now, after more than forty years have passed I love to think of the happy time we had together then.

The War of the Rebellion was going on at that time. We were far from the scene of action and we had no railroad or telegraphic communication with it, still we were deeply interested in it. We took a weekly newspaper, the *New York Tribune,* and we looked eagerly for it each week to learn the war news. Times continued hard with us. The war had interrupted the immigration from the east and there was no market for our produce. We raised good crops but we could not sell our grain for money. Wheat was worth 35 and corn 10 cents per bushel and we had to take trade for it . . . that is, we could not sell it for money.

My husband continued to hunt and trap. In the winter of 1862, he killed a deer, the first one he had seen after we came to this country. It proved to be "dear meat" for him. He went out with his gun one morning and soon got on the trail of a deer. The snow was deep but the excitement of the chase urged him on. He followed it a long distance and finally succeeded in killing it. He skinned it, but cut off only one hindquarter to take home with him; he hung the rest up in a tree. It was then nearly dark and he was several miles from home. It had been snowing all day, and in places the snowdrifts were very deep and he had great difficulty in getting through them. He struggled on and would not abandon the meat he was carrying. He was hungry and the anticipation of delicious venison steak caused him to persevere in holding on to it. When he got home he was nearly exhausted. This brought on an attack of rheumatism and it was several weeks before he was able to go after the meat which he had left hanging in the tree. When he did go after it he found that the wild animals had eaten all of it except the bones.

The winter of 1861–1862 was very cold with lots of snow. I do not think I was away from home all winter, and we seldom had any visitors. The roads were so blockaded with snowdrifts that people did not travel more than necessity compelled them to. My husband's brother Uriah came back from Colorado the fall before and stayed with us that winter.

On April 9, 1862, we moved to our farm which was to be our home for thirty-three years. It did not look much like home when we first moved onto it. It had been rented to a man who was a very poor farmer. The cows, horses, hogs, and geese were all in the dooryard. The house stood on low ground and the melting snow had made it very muddy in the yard and the stock had tramped it into a deep mudhole. The men had to get rails from the fence and make a kind of bridge for me to walk on before I could get into the house. We found that the family had not moved out but were away visiting. We had notified them some time before to vacate the place as their time was out. Therefore we felt free to go in and take possession. It was a cold, windy day. We had come 10 miles in a loaded wagon over bad roads and were all tired and hungry, but we tried to make the best of the situation. Our three little children endured it all bravely without crying. I tried to make them as comfortable as I could and to appear cheerful. It is a great blessing to be able to look on the bright side of life under all circumstances. If a mother can always do this, it brightens up the faces of the little ones and all the members of the family will feel the influence of the sunshine.

The first thing we did after getting into the house was to make a fire. This was not an easy task for there was not a stick of wood or any other kind of fuel to be found. Everything about the yard had been tramped into the mud out of sight. There were a few rails which the renter had not burned on the fence around the field. As soon as one of the men could cut up a rail we built a fire. I had prepared victuals for the occasion and soon had hot coffee and a good dinner ready which made us all feel better. In the evening the renter and his family returned. They had been gone two days and left their stock to take care of themselves. It was about 3 miles to where they had been visiting. They had started home in the morning, but the man had left his family in the wagon on the prairie and went to hunt a colt that had strayed away from home. For that reason it was nearly dark when they returned. I was very sorry for the poor woman and the five little children. Three of them could not walk. The twin babies were only about a month old. The babies were all crying and the mother appeared to be nearly exhausted. I got supper for the family and then tried to quiet the little babies, but I could not. They had been out in the cold wind all day without sufficient clothing, and now they had to suffer for their mother's fault in taking them away from home in such weather and their father's cruel neglect in leaving them out on the prairie so long. One little baby cried nearly all night and after a few days of suffering it was released by death, which in that case surely was a great mercy.

The family with their crying babies moved out the next day after we moved in and I went to work to clean the old house and try to make a home. It was a hard task, but I was young and strong and very hopeful. Now we were on a place of our own, and would not have to move or pay rent which took a large share of our profits.

The mud dried up in the yard, and I made a nice flower garden and planted seed for vines at the windows and about the door. My husband too, went to work to improve the appearance of our surroundings and in a short time it was a very different-looking place.

We had good crops that year, and our stock did well. There was plenty of good pasture on the prairie which was free to all. We milked five cows. I could not make butter to sell because there was no market for it. I made what we wanted to use and fed the rest of the milk to the calves and pigs.

The war was still going on and we were very anxious about the result. The Indians too were a source of anxiety. We often heard rumors of their outrages and many families left this county for fear of them. We did not feel much afraid that they would come and massacre us as they did the settlers in Minnesota. We thought there were too many white settlements between us and the Indian territory for them to make an attack on us. But those were troublesome times and we did not know what might happen.

The Indians came into our neighborhood several times and stole horses. My husband was afraid they would steal ours as they were running loose on the prairie and could easily be caught or driven off. He would take his gun and go out at night and watch for hours. I suffered a great deal from fear that the Indians would kill him while he was out watching the horses. I knew that if they came for the horses that they would not hesitate to shoot him if he interfered with them, and I also knew that he would not let them take his horses without trying to prevent them from doing so. I would lie in bed while he was out and anxiously wait for him to come in, fearing every moment that I would hear the report of an Indian's gun. But they never molested our horses. At one time I was dreadfully frightened. The danger was all imaginary, but I

Along the rivers of Iowa there was plenty of timber. But it had to be converted to lumber for the houses that replaced the log cabins. (1895)

have found that imaginary trials are as hard to bear as real ones. One Sunday morning, five squaws came riding up to our house. They were mounted on Indian ponies and belonged to a tribe of friendly Indians who were on a hunting and begging excursion, but I did not know this at the time. I was unacquainted with Indians and did not know friendly from hostile tribes. My husband asked them if they were camped near and they answered by pointing toward Mason's Grove, which was about a mile distant. We gave them some meat and flour and they rode away. I did not say anything about being afraid, and when my husband said he would go over to the Grove and see if the Indians were there I made no objection. But after he was gone and I was alone with the little children I got uneasy. I thought there might be a band of Indians hiding somewhere near, that they had sent out the squaws to see how the people were situated, and as soon as it was dark that they would attack us.

My husband, not knowing that I was afraid, went over to Mason's Grove where he found a large camp of friendly Indians. As he knew there was no danger of their doing any harm he amused himself watching them at their work and play. The women were busy making baskets, tanning skins, and cooking, while the men pitched quoits, ran races, and engaged in other sports.

In the meantime, I was very anxious. I tried to conceal my feelings from the children, but Byron noticed that I was troubled and he began to be afraid although he was usually a brave little fellow. We were out in the yard about sundown when we saw two Indians carrying guns riding toward the house. The children began to cry and I could bear the suspense no longer. I took baby George in my arms and told Byron and Ida to follow me and we would go to a neighbor's who lived near Mason's Grove. We watched the two Indians as we hurried away, and to our great relief they passed by without noticing us. Still I was afraid there might be others near and that they would attack us after dark. We went on and got to the neighbors just as my husband was riding by on his way home. He was sorry, and surprised that I should have been so frightened. He supposed that I knew that they were friendly Indians and that they were not dangerous. I forgave him but still I thought he did not do right to leave me alone all day when there were Indians around. But we are all liable to do wrong things sometimes. I got on the horse which my husband had ridden, took the baby and Ida on with me. Byron walked with his father. In this way we went home with very different feelings from what we had when we started out.

In the fall of 1862, the hostile Indians again came into the neighborhood, and stole horses. A number of men got together and started in pursuit of them. My husband's brother Uriah took one of our horses to ride and went with them. They overtook the Indians and had a fight. Some of the Indians were wounded but they got away with the stolen horses. Our men had ridden so far and so fast that their horses were nearly exhausted before they came up to the Indians and they were unable to follow them farther. It was fortunate that none of the men were hurt in the fight. There were a number of shots fired from both sides and several horses were wounded. While our neighbors and brothers were away after the Indian horse thieves, word reached us of the Indian massacre of the white settlements in Minnesota. The facts about that horrible event were bad enough. About seven hundred were taken by the Indians, and awful cruelties perpetrated on their helpless victims. But by the time the story reached us it had been greatly exaggerated. There were no railroads or telegraph here then. News had to be passed from one person to another. In this way it grew rapidly until by the time it reached us it was said that the Indians were taking all of Minnesota and northern Iowa, that they were killing the inhabitants and burning and destroying everything they came to. That was the only time I thought there was any real danger of an Indian massacre here. I feared that the Indians had stolen the horses for a ruse to entice our men away from home so that they could come in and plunder the settlement without meeting with serious resistance.

About this time we received a letter from Sister Mary Ellis begging us to move back to Blackhawk County. She thought we were in great danger from the Indians. She said that Brother Hiram's brother-in-law had been killed in the Minnesota massacre. When he heard that the Indians were coming he left everything and took his family to a place of safety. Then he went back to look after his property and was never heard from afterward. His family were left to imagine his fate which no doubt was a cruel death by the Indians.

After reading Sister Mary's letter which contained this sad story my husband wanted me to take the children and go to Sister Mary's and he would stay here and look after our little property.

It was impossible to sell anything here at that time, so many people were leaving, and those who remained were uncertain about their future. No one knew but what they would soon have to flee for their lives.

We could not leave here without sacrificing nearly everything which we had worked so hard to accumulate. I could not think for a moment of leaving my husband here alone exposed to the dangers and to endure the loneliness and hardships of frontier life. I determined to stay with him and await developments and if we had to leave we would all go together.

The Civil War proved to be a much more serious affair than at first it was supposed that it would be. Many thought that it would be an easy task to subdue the rebel lion. It was a common saying that it would only be a before breakfast job to whip the South. But the Bull Run disaster opened the eyes of the people to the greatness of the undertaking. The Indians giving their allegiance to the South made the war more terrible in the West. And then there were many persons in the North who believed that the South had a right to secede, and that slavery was a divine institution and ought to be perpetuated. Those southern sympathizers in the North made the task of subduing the South and the maintenance of our free institutions a much harder task than it otherwise would have been.

We continued to take the *New York Tribune*. It was the only means we had of learning the war news which became more exciting each week. The Sioux Indian war was raging in Minnesota, and the rebels were fighting in Missouri and at one time an invasion of Iowa was expected.

War is a dreadful thing, the innocent suffer with the guilty and cruelty and wrong always accompany it. But sometimes great reforms are accomplished by war which seem impossible to be brought about in any other way. Our Civil War was a purifier of the nation. It was the cause of releasing four million slaves from cruel bondage and of avenging their wrongs. I believe that God the Father heard the cry of his oppressed children and came down in mighty power to deliver them. Our armies gained no decisive battles until President Lincoln declared his intention to free the slaves. After that nearly every battle was a victory for the North. The slaves were praising God for sending them deliverance and their former masters lost courage and soon gave up the conflict.

SORE EYES, THE DRAFT, CLOSE OF THE WAR

The year 1863 makes a thrilling chapter in the history of our country. But it passed very quietly in our little home. We were removed from the fierce conflict which was raging between the North and South. The Indians in Minnesota had been subdued by U.S. troops and we no longer feared depredations from them. But we still felt anxious about the war in the South. During the summer word reached us that the national government had ordered a draft of men to fill the ranks of our armies. This brought the dreadful reality of the war home to every neighborhood in the land.

It was very dry here during the summer of 1863. Some of our neighbors did not raise much corn. It was so dry that the late-planted corn did not come up until the last of June. But my husband planted his corn early (as usual) and it had the benefit of the early rains and we had a good crop. Our stock was increasing in value. We had several head of horses which we had raised and they were in good demand, selling at from one to two hundred dollars apiece. This year we finished paying for our farm which consisted of 80 acres. I had thought when we first contracted for our land that if it was only paid for we would be entirely satisfied. But alas for poor human nature. The more we have the more we want. Earthly possessions never satisfy the immortal soul.

About this time we began to hear of the victories of our northern armies. In July, 1863, President Lincoln issued a proclamation asking the people to observe August 6 as a day of Thanksgiving to God for the turn of the war caused by the victories at Gettysburg and Vicksburg. This tended to restore confidence and to silence the murmurings of some of the people who were tired of the war and wanted peace on any terms, and also to alarm the southern sympathizers in the North.

The winter of 1863–1864 was very cold with some bad blizzards but we had less snow than we had been having every winter before.

After my husband got his corn all gathered and the other fall work done, as usual he spent most of his time hunting and trapping. He killed several deer that winter and I remember that he caught two mink for which he got ten dollars in greenbacks . . . what the paper money was named at that time.

The next spring we all had sore eyes. It was contagious and a dreadful disease. I have never known anything like it since. Nearly everyone in the community was afflicted with it. I greatly feared that some of our children would lose their eyesight. There was no physician near us and I had to doctor them the best I could. We did not entirely recover from the effects of the disease for several years.

In September, 1864, the much dreaded draft occurred in this county. There were twice as many drafted as were wanted. They all had to go to Fort Dodge to be examined as to their physical ability, then one-half of the number were sent home, and the others had to go south to fight for their country. My husband and his brother were both drafted. I bid them a tearful farewell, not knowing whether they would have to go to war or not. It took about one week to go to Fort Dodge and return. That week was one of great anxiety to me. Our corn was not gathered, potatoes dug, or any of the fall work done. We had four little children, the eldest not yet eight years old. I had all that I could do to take care of the children and do the housework without attending to my husband's business. But many a woman was left in as trying circumstances as I would have been, who managed to keep the family together and make a living for them. And in addition to their other hardships they had to bear the suspense of having their loved ones exposed to the dangers of war. Surely our country owes a debt of gratitude to the wives and mothers of its defenders.

Fortunately for us, my husband was rejected, and came home but his brother Uriah had to go to war.

The year 1865 passed without any remarkable event taking place in the family. We worked steadily and made a comfortable living and were accumulating stock and other property. In April of this year word reached us that General Lee had surrendered to Grant and that practically the awful war was over. This caused great rejoicing, but our joy was soon turned into mourning by the news of the assasination of our President whom we had learned to love and honor as we had no other public officer. This cast a gloom over our home and we looked forward to our country's future with dark forebodings. Things were in a very unsettled condition, and we needed just such a wise, strong, and good man as Abraham Lincoln to help reconstruct the Union, and to settle the many vexing questions which arose after the close of the war. But God did not foresake us in our time of need. He raised up other good men to guide our ship of state safely through troublesome times. Our nation still lives. Human slavery is a thing of the past, and we can now truly say that this is "The home of the free, and the land of the brave."

We were still living in the old house which was on the place when we bought it. It was a good-sized frame building but there was only one small room that had been plastered. We had to live in that room during the cold weather and it answered for kitchen, bedroom, and parlor. The other part of the house had only been weather-boarded and the cracks between the boards afforded us plenty of fresh air, and often gave us a good long task of work to shovel out the snow that in time of a storm would drift in. The first warm days of spring, I would go to work and clear this room of the rubbish which accumulated during the winter when we used it for both woodshed and granary. I would sweep down the rough walls, wash the windows, and scrub the floor. As soon as I had cleaned it the best I could, I would move my beds into that room as soon as it was warm enough. I used it for a sitting room. I had beautiful curtains of morning glory vines at the windows and flowers about the door. But I was not entirely satisfied. "Man never *is* but always *to be* blest." I was looking forward to the time when I would have a nice new house. But I had to wait a good while. We were getting a good price for our produce but everything we had to buy was also very high priced. Common unbleached muslin was 50 cents per yard, other dry goods and groceries were equally high. There was no railroad here yet, and we could not get lumber without paying an enormous price for it. And so we worked away earning and saving what we could, and tried to wait patiently until we could get enough to build a comfortable house.

THE RAILROAD

In the year 1866, the Chicago and Northwestern Railroad was built through our county. This brought in a large emigration. Real estate advanced rapidly in value, also all kinds of produce and property. About this time we bought another 40 acres of land. This made a farm of 120 acres. Among the many people who found their way to this county soon after the railroad was completed was a young man named Copeland. He taught our district school and became quite intimate with us. He was from the East, was well educated and had a fine library which he kept at our house, and he gave me the privilege of reading his books. This was a great pleasure for me for I had kept up the habit of reading, but our supply of books was very limited. Among Mr. Copeland's books were Milton's *Paradise Lost,* Longfellow's poems, Walter Scott's romances, and many other works which I read. I wonder now that I found time to read as much as I did. At that time we had five children, and I did all the housework, knit mittens and stockings, and did all the sewing by hand for all the family. I did not have a sewing machine until I had six children. I was young and ambitious. I improved every minute of time and whenever I sat down to hold the baby I always had a book at hand to read. At that time I was almost entirely excluded from society, and I could not go away from home and take so many little children with me, and I stayed at home with them. Books and my family were my world and I was very happy in reading and caring for my children.

SICKNESS, NEW HOUSE

In the fall of 1869, all of the children and myself had the whooping cough. We coughed all winter. When one would commence to cough, all of the others would begin coughing and we would have a lively time for a while. Some of the younger children had it very hard and Lewis, who was the baby then, had the canker-sore mouth and throat in connection and was very ill for a time. He required a great deal of care and as I was coughing hard myself it took all my strength to take care of him and do the work, and wait on the other children. But we managed to get through the winter, and when spring came with its sunshine, birds, and flowers, the children all got well but I continued to cough. The springtime did not bring rest or relief to me. The old house had to be cleaned, bedclothes washed, soap made, and the many other things done which springtime always brings to the farmer's wife. I found that my power of endurance was not equal to the undertaking. My lungs were weak from the effects of the whooping cough. I took cold after washing and coughed worse than I had done in the winter. I found that I had to give up and have a hired girl, but this did not give me much rest. We could not get a competent servant girl, and she made one more in the family and added to my cares. That summer was the hardest time in my life. I had always before, with a few exceptions, had good health, and did not know what it was to be nervous. But now little things worried me, and it was much harder for me to control the children than it had been when I was well and strong.

One evening after the family had retired for the night I was sitting up alone (my cough was worse when I lay down) and was thinking of my situation. I knew I was continually growing worse and unless there was a change soon that I would be beyond help. I thought of my family, each one of them dearer to me than my life. I thought of my boys who so much needed my love and care to direct them in the right way. And my dear little girls, and the baby in my arms. What would become of them if they were left motherless? I became too greatly agitated with these painful thoughts to remain quiet. I went out of the house, and after walking in the yard for some time, I looked up to the beautiful stars above me and thought of their great Creator. A calm came over my troubled heart. I felt that the Father was very near me and I knelt down and asked Him to spare my life to my family. I arose from my knees with a feeling of relief and with an assurance in my heart that my prayer would be answered and that I would get well. The next morning I was worse and scarcely able to leave my bed, but this did not discourage me. I was happy in the firm belief that my prayer would be answered. In a day or two my husband went to Denison to see if he could get anything that would help my cough. There he providentially met a man who told him of a remedy which he said he had known to help persons who had been given up as incurable by their physicians. The following is the recipe for the remedy which cured me:

One ounce of spermaceti shaved fine and mixed with one pound of dark brown sugar and a very little water. Dose: one tablespoon, three times a day.

A few doses helped me, and in a few weeks I regained my health. I have no doubt my strong faith that I would get well had much to do with my recovery for I know that the mind has a great influence over the body.

In the spring of 1870 we began to build our new house and moved into it the next November. It was a nice house for those days in this county. There were eight rooms in it, all nicely finished. The woodwork was all painted except the floors. We did not know then what a blessing a painted kitchen floor is to the tired housewife. I had looked forward to having a comfortable house a long time. We had worked and saved for this purpose. But when we were settled in it, I was not as well satisfied as I had expected to be. We did not have money enough to furnish it as I wished. One thing always calls for another, and I was again reminded of the insufficiency of worldly things to satisfy us.

Our house cost us much more than we had expected. We had to sell nearly all of our stock to pay for it. Up to this time, since the war closed all kinds of farm produce had been high and money was plentiful. But now a reaction set in, and money became scarce and everything depreciated in value. Our family was large and we found it difficult to provide for their numerous wants. But we were much more comfortable than we had been in the old house.

[Asenath Gable's history from this point, 1870, to 1901, when she signed and closed it, is primarily a detailed record of the births of five more sons (plus their characteristics and personalities) and some mention of the great grasshopper plague of the late 1800s. She concludes her story in the high moral sentiment of the day.]

I do not wish for my children a life of ease and unceasing pleasure. But I hope that by industry, economy and perseverance, they will win for themselves an honorable place among men.

And I pray that they may live lives of spotless integrity; that they may always be found the champions of temperance, truth, and righteousness, ever ready to give a helping hand to the unfortunate.

And above all that they may live Christian lives so that we may finally all meet to part no more around our Father's throne in heaven.

Lovingly submitted,

ASENATH GABLE

Denison, Iowa
January 24, 1901

DES MOINES WAS
YOUNG AND GAY

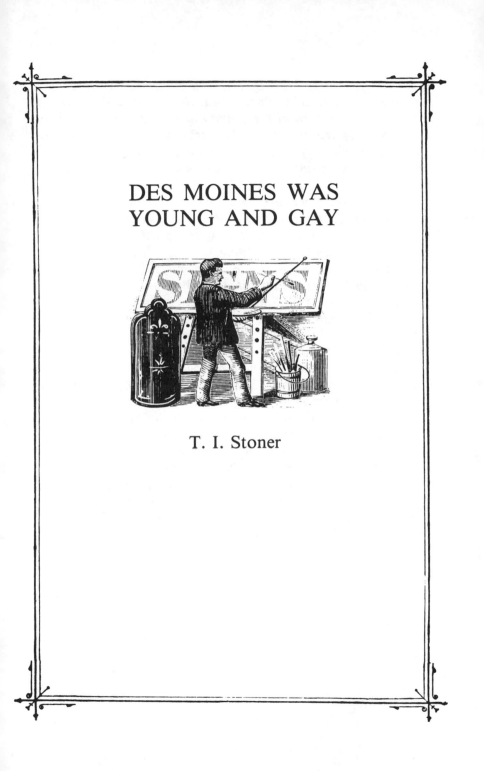

T. I. Stoner

T. I. (TIMMIE) STONER'S STORY could have been ready-made for the old Saturday Evening Post. *It was the motherless urchin growing up at the turn of the century in great poverty who, with boundless determination and energy, steadily mounted the ladder of success, step by step, to become a highly successful and well-known businessman in the capital city of his state, Iowa.*

It is an Iowa story, beginning in the little town of Prairie City and ending only a few miles to the west in Des Moines. But the sixty years which the story spans saw the total transformation of this midwestern state.

Stoner told of that transformation in his privately printed book, In My Time, *published in 1948. With the kind permission of his son, Tom Stoner, a widely known business executive and political figure in the state, we are reprinting excerpts from that book which cover Stoner's early years and the establishment of his first business as a decorator.*

From that modest beginning and Stoner's wide-ranging interests were developed the Stoner-McCray outdoor advertising business, the Stoner Piano Company (because Stoner liked music), and eventually the development in Des Moines—ahead of its time—of the Roosevelt Shopping Center.

You will find the complete story in Stoner's book which you will fully appreciate only when you note his scanty opportunities for education and, finally, the blossoming of this near-destitute youngster into the years of his later success, his love of the arts, his world travels, and the marvels of the opportunities which were his.

ECAUSE of my mother's ill health, we moved to a farm near Prairie City, Iowa, and at that time [1869], I was about one year old. We lived there four years, and they were colorful years. Squaw Creek ran through our farm and the Indians camped nearby. Often they would come to beg. It seemed to my mother, who had so many mouths to feed, that they could smell the aroma of fresh bread for half a mile.

Most of the Indians were friendly. Sometimes, as the Indian children would play near the house by the creek, I would wander down with my little brother at my heels to join in their games. Black Bear, the father of one of the boys, came down on several occasions and tried to talk to me. I liked him and I knew that he liked me.

It was the fall of the year and the kitchen was filled with the pungent aroma of pumpkin butter. Mother used to sweeten it with molasses, and then she would spread some of that delicacy on a slice of fresh home-baked bread! Well, nothing this side of heaven could have tasted half so good. With cheeks flushed from working over a hot stove and pumpkin butter stains on her full checkered apron, mother went to the door to answer a loud knock. There stood a tall Indian with his own little son.

The little fellow, who was about my age, was perched on a white pony. The pony had pink eyes and to me it was the most beautiful creature I'd ever seen.

I looked at the little Indian boy seated so proudly on that beautiful animal and with envy, I wished with all my heart that we could change places. Mother, who was always pleasant with everyone, smiled and asked the Indian what he wanted. "Good day, White Lady," he spoke in a gutteral monotone. He clutched

47

in his hand a string of turquoise beads. "Good day," mother smilingly answered as she dried her hands on her apron, "What can we do for you, Black Bear?" For mother knew this Indian very well since he made almost weekly trips up Squaw Creek—sometimes coming up to our house for the fresh bread but otherwise just sniffing longingly in the direction of the house.

"Me, Black Bear, like your papoose good!" this big Indian said as he pointed to me. "Well, thank you, Black Bear," mother answered, flushing with pleasure, "Silver Star is a mighty fine boy too—he's big and strong and he can ride so well."

"White Woman want trade your papoose for my papoose?" Thinking of possessing that beautiful pony, I looked eagerly up at mother's face for approval. Never shall I forget the expression of incredulity registered there. She couldn't utter a word. "Me give beads, too." Black Bear held out those precious beads that were strung on the dirtiest string I'd ever seen. To me this looked like a good deal for mother, who had never had anything to adorn her lovely neck. I looked hopefully toward her. Then tears suddenly came into her eyes. I saw her shake her head from side to side. Then I felt her arm creep around my shoulder and hold me tightly against her knees.

"Oh no, Black Bear!" she said tremblingly, "Trade off my Timmy! Not for all the pink eyed ponies in the world. Nor all the beads that can be dug out of this earth. You don't know this, Black Bear, so I must tell you—a mother's children are her greatest treasures."

I realized my own mother's reaction and I turned to observe Black Bear. He was standing there with his face extra blank looking, for his face was always blank. He was looking down at his bare feet. Then the magnanimity of my mother grew to boundless heights. She went to the kitchen table, took two large slices of bread, placed heaps of that precious pumpkin butter on each slice and handed them to Black Bear and Silver Star. She closed the door softly then and they padded away down toward Squaw Creek.

Mother silently busied herself with her work. There were no words spoken by either of us. But intuitively I felt she wanted to be alone with her thoughts and I wanted to be alone, too. After those Indians walked down the hill and were out of sight I went to my favorite place at the creek where I'd often played with Silver Star. As I sat there watching the water trickling over the rocks a new understanding was born within me. I'd taken everything my

T. I. STONER

Motherless at an early age, T. I. (Timmie) Stoner grew up in Prairie City, Iowa. With little schooling and his only skill that of a house painter, Stoner began his business career in Des Moines with just 35 cents in his pockets. Subsequently, he became one of the city's major businessmen with investments in many fields.

mother had to offer so terribly for granted. But when she turned down Black Bear's deal, I understood the value she had placed upon me, Timmy Stoner. It suddenly dawned upon me that I'd never had that value in my heart for her. But now I suddenly realized that it took this incident to waken within me this great love which I had for my mother. A minute before a pink eyed pony had meant more to me than anything else in this world. But now I'd suddenly made a brand new appraisal of life's values. Love and devotion are primary. Love and devotion must be the very foundation of life. My mother revealed this to me and I was to base all my future actions upon this foundation of her love for me and mine for her.

☆　　　☆　　　☆

My mother's health did not seem to improve. She worked too hard—there were just not enough hours in the day. And rest? I can never recall seeing my mother rest. When she "rested," she was ill. Father thought perhaps life in town would be less laborious for her so in the spring of the year we moved to Prairie City. Our home was a log house just on the outskirts of town and tucked away in a clump of cottonwood trees. Did you ever hear the wind whistle through cottonwood trees? I still hear sounds that recall those trees and the whistling noise they made.

So many memories come flooding back to me as my mind travels back to life in that little log house. One especially was Saturday night. The old wash boiler was brought into the kitchen and placed by the kitchen stove. Everyone had his turn and we were scrubbed until we shone. Next came the shoes. They were washed, then oiled to keep out the moisture. Five little pairs were lined up for the next week's adventure and five sets of clean clothes were ready for Sunday school the next morning. That was one of the "musts" at our house. "Every good little boy and girl goes to Sunday school," my mother used to say.

☆　　　☆　　　☆

As is the case in most small towns, the general store is the rendezvous for all the farmers who come to town and for the idlers whose only responsibility is to get home at twelve o'clock and at six o'clock to get their stomachs filled. That overstuffed general store in Prairie City was always a revelation to me. They kept everything under the shining sun and I loved to loiter there and listen to the men talk, preferring their company to that of boys my own age. Sitting around on cracker boxes, using the old stove as a spittoon, I would worry lest they would miss their target and, sure enough, frequently they did.

Usually, the stories and yarns were unfit for young ears. But I heard government in all of its ramifications discussed from every angle and such a variety of viewpoints! Many of these men had come from foreign countries and landed here practically penniless. I heard our government granted land to these worthy people who didn't have to be rich; who didn't have to have a legacy; who needed only honesty and integrity to claim the good which came from the land. Of course, they had to work too—and work hard. But they didn't need a thing more than I had at the age of eight years. I used to leave that store with my heart filled with hope. The hope that I, an American, would one day be somebody. Why, I had the makings of this within me. I had the only break an individual needs: to be born. To be born in America. Small wonder that I sought the obscure corner in that group to learn at the feet of these earthy men my first lessons in patriotism and business.

☆   ☆   ☆

That cracker barrel had been filled and refilled many times through the years and always it was allowed to stand open and exposed to the elements, smoke, flies, and human frailties. And the cheese! Large and round like the moon it was when first it rose to the counter. But as the cracker barrel brigade started to file in, the yellow moon began to wane—and fast. Because each member of the brigade during the course of the daily discussion would rise lazily, full of heat and empty of stomach, and sliver off, with a slightly soiled jackknife, a more or less generous slice of the yellow moon. It was amazing how fast that moon waned.

Now, the storekeeper was a good-natured, hard-working individual. He'd have to be to play host to that brigade of loafers who soaked up his heat and utilized his space year after year. But there was a limit to his good-natured endurance. They had no right, these grasshoppers, to eat up his profits. Somewhere through the years there must have been a time of understanding between the loafer and the storekeeper because as each man slivered off his morsel of cheese and reached nonchalantly into the

barrel for crackers, the storekeeper simultaneously reached for his book and wrote down under the account of Jack Jones, we'll say, "Groceries 3c." Or "Jim Johnson, groceries 2c." That bit of good business on the part of my friend the storekeeper made an indelible impression on me. For this was the *real* reason for my being found here constantly among the members of the cracker barrel brigade. It wasn't the tobacco juice, or the savory stories of the town gossip that fascinated me—it was the store itself. I loved everything about it.

☆   ☆   ☆

One day my father decided he would take a trip to Omaha and that I should accompany him. Never having seen anything outside of Prairie City and the surrounding country, it was a glorious adventure. Those hills around Council Bluffs looked like

As a small boy, T. I. Stoner's experiences in main street stores fired his imagination to make his way in the world. A typical hardware store and a drug store-soda fountain as they appeared in the early 1900s. (1913)

huge mountains. "Why, this is traveling, seeing the world and how much fun it is. Some day, I will go clear out to California." I confided my thoughts to my father. He didn't seem to share my enthusiasm at all. "Son," he said, "you would have just about as much chance to take a trip out to California as to the planet Mars."

It was exciting walking about the streets of Omaha, seeing the sights. It was such a big city and there was so much to see. There were many, many Indians loitering about. Of course, I was used to the Indians along Squaw Creek but they weren't so colorful as these Indians. They didn't wear such attractive beads, have such beautiful blankets, or such an array of handsome feathers.

Father was looking for buffalo robes and there were plenty of them for sale. They were piled out in front of stores, layer on layer of them. Finally, after much looking and much talking, he purchased two. One, he paid $12 for and the other $13. They were fine robes and father felt satisfied with the price. One of these robes had an important function to perform. It was to hang between the two rooms of our little log house where a door should have been. Those were all the rooms there were—with the exception of a loft and, of course, that was where we children slept.

We were not allowed to have a candle in the loft. In fact, much of the time there were no candles. They were not readily available, for one reason or another, so very often our only means of light was a pan with grease in the bottom. In that was a rag—the end of which was lighted, and that was it—all the light we had.

When it came bedtime, when the days were short, father would stand with his head just under the hole which went into the attic. He was tall and he held the pan high while the five of us would scamper up the ladder to bed. The light in father's hand would make strange and grotesque figures on the walls and we would hurry across the cold floor to our beds and frantically pull the covers over our heads. Often, in the winter, the snow would drift in through the rafters but we were young and rugged.

There is no single period of my life that I have retrospected over so much as the time in which we lived in the little log house. We were all together then, all of us. The ties were as yet unbroken. I seem to remember all the intimate little details. The whole picture stands out like a precious cameo.

☆   ☆   ☆

My mother's health, which was always delicate, was growing steadily worse. I was seven and didn't realize this terrible fact. She called me to her bedside one morning. "Timmy, my little man," she said as she hugged me close to her, "Soon, too soon, I won't be with you. I'll have to leave you, Timmy." My young mind could not comprehend her meaning. I turned and looked at her in surprise. "Why, where are you going, mother?" I asked. She tried to tell me about death. I couldn't comprehend this condition and I had had no experience with this finality known as death. Though I had grown used to her frailties—the hours she had lain on her bed, the pink cheeks that only added to her cameo-like beauty—yet I finally understood the truth; my grief knew no bounds. Or did I really understand? Is it possible for any child of eight to know the utter vacuum one experiences in losing his best friend, his mother, for she passed on in only a few days after this little talk.

☆   ☆   ☆

Besides father, there were five of us to mourn her passing. Jim, Rosie, Flora, Royal, and I. Rosie and Flora were taken by relatives and the rest of us attempted to keep "bachelor's hall." We left the log house and took up quarters in an old, vacated store building in Prairie City. How vacant and barnlike it looked! A woman who loves her family can take a barn and make a home of it—but what could a bereaved man with his three little boys do?

We took stock of what we had and made the best of our lot. Jim, who soon was old enough to shift for himself, found a job in the country. That left father, Royal, and me.

☆   ☆   ☆

Along about six-thirty o'clock father, who was doing a repair job on some buildings near town, would come along with some bologna and we would boil some potatoes, and call it a day.

We would have gotten along fairly well at that had I not taken typhoid fever. There were many in the town who had it. The only nursing I had was what little Royal could give me by day and father by night. Quinine in those days was given straight—no sugar-coating—no capsule. For so long nothing mattered, getting well or not—it was all the same, not important. Slowly my strength came back and I thought of the future. Why of course, the future! My ambition to have a general store all my own and, yes, the white pony! Besides all that, father had told me just the week before that I was his partner and that he was depending on me. Yes of course it mattered—everything mattered! Yes, I must get well—and I did.

☆   ☆   ☆

March first is moving time in rural communities and about this time the Stoners received a letter! To receive a letter was an event. The postmaster called me into the office and handed me this letter addressed to my father. I hurried to the place where he was repairing a roof. He dropped hammer, saw, nails, and boards and rushed down to get the letter. I watched with bated breath while he opened it.

"Humph!" said my father and got no further. I pretty nearly popped. "Humph!" he said again—but I dared not interrupt.

"Well," he folded the paper and replaced it in the envelope. "Well, Tim, I guess we'll be moving." I studied his face—a bright new light seemed to rest there.

"What's up, father?" I couldn't stand the suspense any longer.

"The letter's from your sister, Rosie." Father smiled, "She wants us all to live together again out on the farm—she says she'll keep house for us. And Jim's coming back, too, to give me a hand on the farm. Get home now and start packing up. The Stoners are moving."

Rosie was now sixteen. She was shy, sensitive, and there were times when her two younger brothers were too much for her. There were many humorous and near tragic incidents, but, as a whole, life was pleasant and there was good food once again. Our aunt had taught Rosie how to cook. How our mouths would water when we would come filing into the kitchen and smell the freshly baked beans with salt pork and see the corn pone all ready and steamy hot for dinner. And even apple pie, once in a while, as a nice surprise!

☆   ☆   ☆

For about two years the Stoners lived together in this fashion. Royal and I receiving our education; Jim helping father with the various tasks to be done on a farm; and Rosie keeping us well fed in an admirable fashion.

Then one evening after the work of the day had been completed and we boys had gone off to bed, Rosie sat down beside father and shyly told him she wished to marry. A few weeks later a young man came to take Rosie away with him. They drove off in an old democrat wagon with a horse that had seen better days. We stood at the gate waving to them until the second hill hid them from view.

We stood a moment looking into the empty distance. Then the four of us turned and looked dejectedly at our father. I'd never seen this expression in his eyes before. "Well," he said uncertainly, "I guess that's the end of our home life."

"Yes, father," said Jim slowly, "I guess it is. Anyway, it ends it for me because Samuel Patterson asked me yesterday if I'd like to have my job back that I left two years ago when I came to live here on the farm. I think I'd better take it."

"I do too, Jim," father said as he placed his hand on Jim's

shoulder. Then I saw Royal slip his little hand into father's. "And you're going to leave me too, Royal. You'll be happy with your auntie. And Tim and I will go back to Prairie City."

By trade, my father was a carpenter and contractor. He wanted me to help him and indeed I would have done anything to help. I was only a boy but I was already in a heavenly radiance of anticipation. I was learning many things . . . how to shingle; how to lath; and how to do many of the simple jobs in construction work.

Then came my last chance for more schooling. Father succeeded in getting me in to live with the Harry Griffith family. However, after I had finished the seventh grade, I discovered that further education was a luxury the Stoners could not afford and I started to shift for myself. At every opportunity I would work—picking apples, digging potatoes, and anything to earn a little money and a good, hot meal. Food was at a premium in those days and it seemed that I was always hungry.

Father's work took him often to the country and to nearby towns so I had to learn to shift for myself. It was at this period of my life I took up bootblacking in Prairie City—just a small town, but in those days it was even smaller, about three hundred souls. That didn't make many shoes to shine; because there were very few of that number who could afford to have their shoes polished, and a few who could, didn't care to. Life was simple, and there were few occasions for which to have one's boots dressed up.

Times were hard indeed. There was very little money in the country and food wasn't plentiful, at least, so it seemed to me. It may sound like a chapter out of *Les Miserables* when I record that the roof over my head during that time was an old vacant house—not haunted, except that it might have had those reactions to a young, impressionable boy of twelve. I can remember how very dark that room was and the howling of the wind, the quaking of the building on stormy nights. I remember how I would snuggle deeper into the old quilts I had found to cover me, but I was thankful there was a roof over my head and that the rain couldn't get in. It might have, at that, had not I chucked some old rags into the hole where a pane had fallen out.

In this old building, which had at one time been a hotel, we had stored our only worldly goods. The prize possession was the buffalo robe which my father had bought in Omaha and had hung in the doorway of the old log house. Yes, I was thankful for a place where I could find rest and refuge . . . where I could dream

about town I came upon an uncle of mine who lived in Prairie City. When I found him, he was repairing a picket fence. He was putting new boards in to replace the old worn ones. The fence looked ugly. Part of it new, part of it black where the elements had played. Then a miracle happened! With a brush and some snow white paint it all looked the same. He was turning an ugly, old fence into something uniform, something beautiful. I was thrilled. I, too, wanted to paint—and when my uncle asked me if I wanted a job—I could hardly wait to get hold of the brush. What a job! Why at that moment of enthusiasm I would have worked for nothing—and it eventually proved that I had. For in the language of Bob Burns, the Arkansas traveler, "He was my drinkin' uncle." No, I never was paid for my work, but at least through this experience I found a new line of work, work at which I could earn my living. For this reason, I should, and do, feel kindly towards him.

☆   ☆   ☆

Down through the centuries the circus has been dear to the heart of every boy. I was no exception. The more I looked at those gaily colored poster boards with the lions roaring at me, the more determined I was to see the coming circus. The posters read, "Seats as low as twenty-five cents." I managed to save a quarter but to get to Des Moines was something else. Spring wagons and buggies were the only means of transportation. My chum was as eager to go as I and hearing of six men who had hired a wagon we asked if we might ride.

There was no room except under the spring seats but those spaces were offered to us. We were to start at four-thirty in the morning to avoid the crowds. As we were not paid passengers we decided to take no chances on getting left. The night man at the livery barn was a kindly fellow and we asked him if we couldn't bunk there for the night. Maybe he had boys of his own. Anyway, he was a swell guy. We climbed up into the loft with some old horse blankets to keep us warm, but sleep wouldn't come.

☆   ☆   ☆

At the appointed time the six men appeared. My chum and I crawled under the seats and we were off on the biggest adventure of our lives, to see our first circus. It was a long, dusty ride but an

The first Savery Hotel, 1888–1918, was a major Des Moines edifice when T. I. Stoner was venturing into the capital city. Built at an estimated cost of $250,000, it was advertised as "the finest between Chicago and San Francisco."

eager, enthusiastic boy of thirteen thought little of cramped muscles and a dirty face. At last we arrived. The crowd was immense. I proudly stepped up to buy my ticket, producing my 25 cents. Gruffly the man pushed me aside and said, "No 25 cent seats." Quickly I thought, "Those beautiful bill boards and they didn't tell the truth." I sat down to think. My stock was a little low just then. Then along came a big, burly looking fellow carrying a neck yoke and double tree. My utter dejection must have touched him. I am sure my face was several shades darker than it should have been, after that long, dusty ride and I was tired and hungry. Little wonder that I looked forlorn. Anyway there must have been something about this small boy's appearance that touched the man. "What's the matter, kid. Wanta git in the circus and ya ain't got no money, eh?" "Oh, yes," I answered, proudly showing him my quarter, "but they wouldn't let me in for 25 cents." He looked at the quarter, handed it back to me and said, "Here, kid, take this rope and bucket and move right along with me." He lifted the canvas and we walked under the tent. Oh, such a big tent, such a crowd and so much to see! I turned to my blessed benefactor with deep gratitude. "Thank you, sir, for being so good to me." "That's all right, kid, but just hand over that quarter to me." I did, I turned to look at the animals, I turned quickly back to him—but he was gone.

The circus was all that any boy could ask. The return trip was a blur in my mind because my friend and I slept all the way home to Prairie City. However, I awakened the next morning to stern realities of earning a living for myself.

☆   ☆   ☆

It was the summer of 1882. I had heard that there was to be a new lodge building erected in Runnels and I lost no time in soliciting a job. The contractor looked me over and said, "Tim Stoner's your name, eh? Well, if your muscles stuck out a little more maybe you could carry brick and mortar for me. 'Fraid you're a little small, though, boy." Small! Why even I didn't know my own strength. I picked up a large pail of mortar and held it way up just to show him I was no weakling. He gave me the job, but before the day was over I felt maybe the boss was right. Perhaps I was a little light for such heavy work. However, no one showed me any favoritism because of my size and I worked right along with the others. The building had an exceptionally tall chimney on it, in fact, it looked large enough to accommodate a good-sized Santa Claus. It was my job to carry the brick and mortar and I did, up to the last brick and pail. Across the street a druggist, who, when he wasn't busy selling asafetida and sassafras tea, would stop and watch the crew work. He evidently took note of those who were the faithful ones and those who were just clock workers. Anyway at the close of my third day's work he came over and engaged me in conversation. "Any job after you leave this one, son?"

"Nothing in sight," I answered.

"I wonder if you would be interested in whitewashing some schoolhouses. The township is pretty well broke, I understand, and you may have to take due bills. If you do, I'll cash 'em for you. I understand they will pay only $3 per schoolhouse. Always glad to help an ambitious kid."

☆   ☆   ☆

Whitewashing schoolhouses was a brand new kind of work, and I liked it. One of the boys, Charles Kesteven, who was working on the lodge building also, decided he wanted to go into partnership with me in whitewashing the schoolhouses. That night, in a dingy restaurant over our evening meal, we made our plans. First we had to have tranportation. We were able to hire a spring wagon and a team for $1.50 per day. The lime would cost us 10 cents and the bluing 5 cents for each schoolhouse.

My partner and I were as happy as the larks that sang along the roadside we traveled. By working twelve hours and with careful manipulation, we succeeded in completing two schoolhouses each day, thus netting us $2.10 each, per day.

Our last job was in the Garrett district, and my partner and I were in a merry mood. Whether or not neighbor Garrett heard our lusty voices singing out the latest tunes, I don't know, but as we looked out of the open window we saw Mr. Garrett, who was blind, being led up onto the front stoop. He had just come over for a little friendly visit, and he wished to compliment us on our fine work. We couldn't, however, become too conceited with his compliments, in view of the fact that the man could see nothing. Anyway it was pleasant to hear him say, "Boys, I hear you two are hustlers and I want you to come over to my place for supper and spend the night."

Being guests of the Garretts, my partner and I could hardly

take the liberty of saying to our host, "Mr. Garrett, your buildings look like paint hasn't yet been invented." No, we couldn't say that. However, before the evening was over, I am afraid propriety did take wings, because I remarked, "Mr. Garrett, you have a beautiful place here, and with a little work done, your farm would be the envy of all the countryside." I am convinced that people have pride even though they cannot see. Then too, I shall always think that a certain pretty schoolteacher who boarded there at that time helped me to put the deal across. The house was painted first and that made the barn look drabber than ever. Consent was given to paint the barn. Then the machine shed and other buildings looked grotesque by comparison. Building after building was treated to a new coat of paint until all were uniform. The job really looked beautiful, and as a result we enjoyed a season of work right in that locality.

This little rural community had its own social life and Charles and I were soon asked to their parties. We danced, usually to the tune of a fiddle or an organ, and sometimes both. Never do I hear "Turkey in the Straw" that I don't think of those nine schoolhouses, old blind Garrett, and the parties we enjoyed. We would dance until the hours were small, then refreshments were served. Molasses candy, popcorn balls, frosted cakes, fresh cider, and coffee. Then a long walk home, or if we were fortunate, a ride in a lumber wagon or a hayrack. But walk or ride it didn't matter too much. Life was good and those were truly the good old days.

☆　　　☆　　　☆

Always the grass looks greener on the other side of the fence. Des Moines, which I had been privileged to see only a few times, loomed up as a great and wonderful metropolis to my young eyes. I felt I had acquired considerable experience and that I was ready to get out into the great, wide, wonderful world and do things.

☆　　　☆　　　☆

It was the year 1885 and Des Moines had a population of about 50,000. Des Moines' tallest building was the Van Ginkel building, located just across from the Savery Hotel. It was twelve stories high.

After surveying the town, I called at Harvey and Grandeur, who were then the leading decorators, and applied for a job. For a year I worked for this firm during which time I acquired valuable knowledge in the art of decorating. Working for these decorators was very satisfactory, but always there was the urge to be in business for myself. The small amount of money I was able to save that year was indeed inadequate to enable me to hang out my own "shingle." Yes, I must go to a smaller place. Just how or why one makes a certain decision to locate in this place or that, has always been a puzzle to me. For some strange reason I commenced to look towards Nebraska. Perhaps it was that trip I had made to Omaha with my father, years before when I was a very young boy.

Council Bluffs was a thriving steamboat terminal and an outfitting town. It had been selected, way back in 1862, as the eastern terminus of the Union Pacific Railroad. It was really an important city. Beyond Omaha lay the plains of Nebraska. I had heard of Valley—the name seemed to stick in my memory. Valley, Nebraska, that was the place where I would go. So with Brother Jim and a good racing pony, we commenced the journey to our objective. The population of this small town was only a few hundred and it lay beautifully cupped in the Platte Valley.

In choosing Nebraska as our particular frontier we felt we were going west, because that state was considered "West" in those days. No period is a pioneering period as one goes through it, it only becomes so as one has left it.

One of the advantages of living in Valley, Nebraska, in those early days was that it didn't cost much. Corn sold for 8 cents a bushel; potatoes cost 28 cents a bushel; eggs 6 cents a dozen. One of the distinct disadvantages, however, was the low wages paid to workers then. So while it didn't cost much to live, there was real difficulty in finding even the small amount of money it did take to buy actual necessities.

One of the astonishing things about youth, however, is that when one finds it necessary to work for his very existence he seems to acquire the physical capacity needed for that exertion. And my brother Jim and I expended plenty of physical exertion making a living. As I look back now upon those days, I wonder how we put in the long hours during the two years we lived in Valley, Nebraska. But we never seemed to think of this experience as a hardship.

☆   ☆   ☆

We worked! We made some money, too. A lot of business we did was "put on the books" but I made enough to clear my credit when we sold our building. After I paid my debts, I was again without funds; and except for the money that other people owed me I had no resources. I decided I needed more education. Having been forced to leave school at such an early age, I felt that my education was inadequate to carry on a business career.

I learned that tuition at Shenandoah Normal College was less than at other schools which I had been considering. And I certainly had to consider capital because a good many of our painting jobs "on the books" were not paying out very fast. Father offered to lend me $100, which was to be paid back from collections from the old book accounts. In the finals, however, the collections did not meet my requirements and as a result at the end of eight weeks I was compelled to leave school and again find employment and replenish my depleted funds.

Eight weeks of additional education may seem a short time, but by applying myself diligently I succeeded in securing the award for being second in improvement during my stay at the college. Besides getting the fundamentals of a business course, I made the acquaintance of fellow students and professors, some of whom later developed into prominent citizens in other localities.

☆   ☆   ☆

It was during the fall of 1889 that I returned to Des Moines. I was again seeking employment. I walked the streets—I had no money for carfare—looking everywhere for work. My feet were sore for days from walking so far. I had no easy time locating a job.

In spite of the fact that Des Moines was growing, work was not easy to find. I knew the town was growing because a report from Persingers' Times in December, 1886, had stated: "The record of Des Moines has been a remarkably bright one despite the scarcity of capital. On the threshold of a new national administration, the tumultous and menacing labor eruptions last May, the alleged blighting influence of prohibition in Iowa, and the chronic cry of 'hard times,' the improvements in Des Moines in 1886 have reached up into the millions."

I read and digested the facts in this report. I believed them, too, for I saw that building was going forth rapidly in this town. Where there is building, there is work for decorators. I decided that Des Moines was my city, and it was here that I would stay and cast my lot. The population of the town was carried about in

T. I. Stoner felt sorry for the horses which powered the Des Moines mass transit system for a period of 20 years. This was 1886.

streetcars drawn by horses. The driver would sit out on the "front porch," so to speak, with a round-wheeled brake between his knees, and control the speed so that on hills and difficult places the car wouldn't run into the horses. The poor animals had a hard time of it, always having sore feet. This was the result of running between the tracks and constantly hitting their feet on the rails. I always felt a bond of sympathy and understanding for these brutes—their feet hurt and so did mine.

The horses wore bells on them to let the pedestrians know they were coming and to give them time to get to the corner. These streetcars went up Walnut until they came to Ninth Street. I used to walk from Twenty-eighth and Grand to Eleventh and University. The horse-drawn streetcars moved so slowly that I usually beat their time, and besides that, which was of major importance, I saved a nickel.

In seeking a job, I found one with the Holland New Company. With but 35 cents in my pocket it came just in time. This company had a good reputation and exacted careful work from its employees, which was indeed good training for me. One of the first houses in which I worked was the E. E. Clark home located at 401 Twenty-eighth Street. Mr. Clark was the second president of Bankers Life Company and a gentleman of merit.

☆   ☆   ☆

Mrs. Clark had always been kind and helpful to me and many a job which I was successful in getting I traced to her generous recommendations. One of the last jobs I worked on for this firm was the Bird Schoolhouse at Harding Road and Woodland Avenue. It was a big job and many were employed on it. Across the street there was a well and also a house in which lived a pretty widow. I never to this day have seen such a dry bunch of workers. Someone was continuously leaving and getting a drink. I couldn't understand why, if an employer was fair to his help, the help wouldn't reciprocate in like manner. The men were also careless with their brushes, and I found them at the end of a job here and there all over the place.

It was Saturday and all day I had thought about quitting and when the whistle blew my decision was made. I walked up to Mr. Holland, handed him the brushes I had found, and told him I had decided to go into business for myself.

One day, as I was walking past Dr. LeRoy's home (and it still stands at the northeast corner of Sixteenth and Linden), I noticed how badly it needed painting, so I knocked at the door. Before I left the house I had made a deal which was satisfactory to both of us. I was to paint the house, and as remuneration I was to get the doctor's old horse, the horse he had used in his practice for years. To be sure, old Bessie had sore feet but with care she would give me a lot of service. Mrs. LeRoy wiped away a tear or two as I led old Bessie away. Bessie had been such a part of their family life that my adopting her made a strong bond of friendship between us, and the LeRoys were always my friends.

Now I had a horse, I must find a wagon. About a week later I saw a sign in a yard "wagon for sale." I had no money but I did have a watch and chain. My father had given it to me and I was very proud of it. I hesitated only a moment, because well did I know that this was not time for sentiment. So I handed the precious timepiece to the owner of the wagon and asked him if he would trade. We both knew that he got the better of the deal. It was five years before I again owned a watch. In the year of 1894 my employees presented me with a beautiful Elgin with this inscription: "Presented to T. I. Stoner by his employees. Christmas 1894."

It was indeed a humble place where I put up my first shingle. The location was 509 Mulberry Street north of the Courthouse.

T. I. Stoner's first place of business was in a basement shop at 509 Mulberry. He traded a gold watch given him by his father for his first wagon and the horse (with sore feet) was pay for a painting job he had done.

The space I had selected was a basement room. There was no floor because long before it had rotted away. The only redeeming feature of the place was the price, which was reasonable enough, being only $5. The building was owned by ex-Mayor Campbell who operated a printing shop on the first floor. Mr. Campbell was both generous and good natured and he trusted me for my first month's rent. Humble though my place of business was, the sign which I hung above it was neat and dignified. "T. I. Stoner, Decorator."

Yes sir, that sign looked attractive to me, but I knew all too well that business just doesn't come to you. It was up to me to get out and get it. This I did. In fact, I was out of my shop most of the time. I began to wonder if I wasn't missing a lot of calls that my sign must be attracting to the store. What I needed was an office boy to help me catch that business. I soon found one in the person of Robert Thompson. He was given instructions to get the name of any and every prospective customer who came through my door. I left him in charge of my new decorating "studio." Next morning, confident that my interests were protected, I spent a long, hard day out of the office. At six o'clock I came in, threw my cap on the counter and turned to Bob. "Any customers, Bob?" I asked hopefully.

"Oh yes," Bob replied enthusiastically. "There were several men in."

"Get their names?" I asked.

"No," Bob answered nonchalantly. "They said they knew you and they'd all be back later."

I could readily see that the service Bob Thompson was going to render me would be extremely unsatisfactory. This I told him. He left my shop for another job. I purchased a 10 cent slate and tied a piece of chalk to it. I printed a little sign above it which read: PLEASE PUT YOUR NAME HERE.

The slate brought me plenty of names and addresses. I discovered, however, that a lot of the names were phoney ones written by neighborhood pranksters and many a trip I made to run down possible business was fruitless. However, most of the names I found on my little slate in the evening after a hard day's work were prospective customers. Years later I met this same Robert Thompson whose job my slate had filled. We were at some entertainment together. He mentioned the incident to me and said, "That was rather a tough lesson you taught me when I was your office boy, Mr. Stoner, but believe me I've benefited by it."

Streetcars came to Des Moines in the period which T. I. Stoner remembered as being "young and gay." (1910)

*Des Moines welcomes
President William Howard Taft.
(1909)*

☆　　　☆　　　☆

Back in the nineties Des Moines was young and gay. The early pioneers were practical, however, in respect to their building programs and in their outlook for the future of the city.

It was natural that the main street of Des Moines would be Grand Avenue. And the Grand Avenue of the nineties was a very different looking thoroughfare than it is today. It was not paved with cement. It was covered with round cedar blocks. The hoofs of the horses, as they trotted down the Avenue, made a soft sound

on these paving blocks. And Grand Avenue had the distinction of being the elite street of the town. There were no tall buildings—insurance or otherwise—no funeral homes, no oil stations on the Avenue of that day. Beautiful homes had been and were being erected on this street. In the rear of these homes there was not the customary garage of today. However, each home maintained a stable where horses and surreys—with or without the fringe on top—were kept. It was a common sight to see a surrey, pulled by a perfectly matched team of bays, dashing down the street, nickle-plated harnesses glistening in the sunlight.

The occupants within the surreys were usually a handsomely dressed man, and sitting beside him would be Milady attired in a heavy silk, hoop-skirted gown and holding a tiny lace trimmed parasol over her head if the day were sunny and the carriage top down. And these attractive persons were undoubtedly members of the smart set of the Des Moines of that day.

For Des Moines had her social smart set and through the patronage of these wealthy families the theater thrived. Going to the theater was a great social event. The fashionable patrons were usually driven there by a uniformed "man" and left at the entrance of the theater. The ladies would be gorgeously gowned and the men were no less handsome in their toppers and black capes lined with white satin. The Foster House was a very popular theater, and there was the Bijou (which was burlesque). This theater was operated by Madame Reinhart, where I remember seeing the dog-faced boy, the fat woman, and the thin man—all for 10 cents! Billy Moore's theater was located at Fourth and Walnut Streets. However, the most fashionable theater was the Grand Opera House. It was in this Opera House that the best shows appeared. Des Moines was even then known as a good "show town" and it is today. Many famous names appeared on the billboards of the Grand Opera House: Maude Adams, Tim Murphy, Edwin Booth, Frederick Paulding, Mata Creigon, and Madame Modjeska were only a few of the topflight actors and actresses at that time. I remember when Ethel Barrymore played a role of parlormaid with her famous father as the lead in the show called "The Stroke of Twelve." "Faust" was played in this theater and another show which received a great ovation, known as "Lost in New York," I especially remember.

☆   ☆   ☆

For more than sixty years Des Moines has been my home. I have seen it grow from the horse-drawn trolley cars to curbliners which noiselessly glide along our streets today in this year of 1948. There have been great changes in this city during my time.

In outdoor advertising, as well as in other ways, T. I. Stoner's name became known all over Iowa. Here a Stoner-McCray workman puts up a war bond sign during World War II.
(1942)

In 1934 T. I. Stoner built the Roosevelt Theater and the accompanying shopping center, decades before the age of shopping centers. The site, Stoner recalled, was "just a frog pond." The project, costing $60,000, was the largest in Des Moines in 1934–1935. Twelve thousand people attended the opening.

What will be our progress in the next sixty years? Looking through my mental binoculars I can see great and good things ahead for my city and state and nation and world. Peace is the prayer of our world. Our thinkers imply that the road to peace lies through the door of education for all peoples of all nations. If this be truth, then it is my fervent prayer that a worldwide educational program will be launched which will bring the light of truth to every man, woman, and child in every nation. I believe that in the light of truth our children and their children will move out and progress on the firm ground of faith.

Oliver Wendell Holmes spoke truly when he said of Americans of the past: "Too often we are moved and motivated by our fears rather than by our faith." I believe our children are heading out toward higher ground, for they are moving confidently out in the light of truth motivated by faith such as our old world has never before known.

MEMORIES
NEVER FORGOTTEN

C. V. Findlay

C. V. FINDLAY'S IOWA ROOTS were first put down in 1870, in northwest Iowa, Clay County, where his parents were homesteading. Subsequently, he moved to Webster County and began an illustrious career. He taught school, was county superintendent, president of Tobin College in Fort Dodge, farmed, raised a family, was a member of the Fort Dodge Council and later mayor, prominent state churchman, and served in both the Iowa House and Senate for extended periods. He died in 1951 at the age of eighty-five.

In retirement Findlay turned to recording his pioneer experiences for immediate members of his family. One copy is now carefully preserved in the Fort Dodge Library.

From a son, James F. Findlay of Springfield, Missouri, we have permission to reprint a few of the original sketches. Findlay, for some reason, chose to speak in the third person. We have taken editorial license and recast his recollections in the first person.

THE FINDLAY FAMILY COMES TO IOWA

I was born at Paw Paw, Illinois, where my father was farming. Our family had heard about the West and decided they wanted to go there. So in 1870 we started for Iowa along with another family, an uncle.

Father had three horses and my uncle had one, so the two families came in two covered wagons, moving along slowly, hindered by poor roads and bad weather. We camped when nightfall came.

We crossed the Mississippi River at Dubuque on a ferry. We passed through Clear Lake where we found a few houses on the bank of the of the lake and finally came to Algona. This was the farthest point west that the Milwaukee Railroad had reached then. We had no definite place we wanted to go, so on and on we went. We had heard stories of beautiful lakes in northern Iowa, surrounded with wooded areas. These stories kept us pushing on. We went as far as Trumbull Lake where the two men decided they were pleased with the prairie. Father and uncle looked around for several days and then went to Spencer, the county seat, where they entered a homestead claim for two 80-acre tracts of land.

We took the wagon boxes with their white coverings off the wagons and set them on the ground. These were to be the homes of the two families for a time. The men started for Algona which was 40 miles away. They were going there to buy lumber and would be gone a week.

Imagine two unprotected women alone with six children out on that vast Iowa prairie! Such an experience called for true heroism.

AN OLD-TIME BLIZZARD

One winter we had been having beautiful weather for several days. A beautiful snowfall of a foot or more had covered everything. It had remained where it fell. We had been burning hay for fuel all winter. One day father said that he would go to Estherville, a distance of 14 miles, and get a load of wood.

The morning he left the sun rose bright. This lovely winter day continued well into the afternoon. Then fleecy clouds began to appear. They quickly settled down into a solid bank on the western horizon.

Mother began to wonder about the sudden change and hurried to feed the chickens before it should get dark. After hurriedly feeding the stock, mother brought a rope from the stable. She fastened one end to the stable door. She unwound it as far as it would go. Then she hurried to get her clothesline to lengthen it. She then tied the other end to the door of the house. It was this act which no doubt saved her life.

Scarcely had she finished when a great, white, solid wall of snow, reaching from the earth to the clouds, appeared in the northwest. It came on with the speed of a racehorse and with a deep, moaning, groaning, rumbling sound which struck terror and fear into the boys who had never seen such a monster. Back of its swiftly moving front, everything instantly vanished from sight.

This was the northwest blizzard that attacked our sodhouse with a fury that cannot be described. During that night and the day and night following and through another day and night there was not the slightest letup in the storm's fury.

Father had provided us with a large supply of twisted hay for fuel. Mother realized that there was danger we might run out in such a furious storm.

The rope to the barn was a great help to mother because she could follow it to the stable and find her way back to the house with it. Without it she would have been lost. The family managed to stay warm, but we ran low on food. The boys were put to work grinding corn in the coffee mill. They had to grind it several times to get it fine enough to be made into cornbread or mush. Our wise mother knew her children would not starve on johnnycake made of meal ground in a coffee mill.

Father had hurried to cut the load of wood and had started home. He was out from Estherville a few miles when the storm struck him as suddenly as it had the sodhouse. He was helpless.

C. V. Findlay was four years old when his family, by team and wagon, came to northwest Iowa. In the subsequent eighty-one years before his death, he grew up as a boy on the prairies and rose to positions of importance in Iowa government and politics.

He just let the horses go where they would, putting all his trust in them. He grasped the end of a stick in the load and followed behind, not knowing where he was going. They went on several miles with father not being able to see the load of wood before him. The team stopped suddenly, and father went to learn what was the trouble. The team had stopped at a stable made of hay and father knew it was useless to try to go farther. He found room inside for his team and cared for it. He did not know where he was or whose barn he had entered. He had no idea which direction the house was from the stable. He saw a dog in the barn. So he opened the door and drove the dog out. He watched the direction the dog went and followed. He found the house in this way which was lucky for both him and the people in it. Their father had gone to Estherville for wood and needed food and he, too, was lost in the storm. The family was without food of any kind and had only frozen potatoes for food. Father managed to bring in his wood, stick by stick. This was the fuel that kept them from freezing. After father had been there several hours, another man found the door and knocked. The man was the owner of the house who had found his way to his own home. During the three nights and days, they burned both loads of wood. They did not complain that they had only frozen potatoes to eat.

The morning of the third day the storm stopped as suddenly as it had begun. But the temperature was very low, and it was terribly cold. Mother began to scan the horizon, hoping someone would appear—most of all her husband. By this time we realized what danger we had been through and we, too, scanned the horizon anxiously. In a prairie region one could see as far as the eyesight could reach. Finally we saw a team come into sight away to the northwest. We were overjoyed when we were sure it was father.

Father had walked behind the sled, but in spite of his efforts, his feet were frozen as was every exposed part of his face. He could never get over wondering how he had escaped being frozen to death. From that time on father dreaded being away from home.

THE GRASSHOPPER PLAGUE OF 1876

In these early days of homesteading there were no fences. It was necessary to watch the cattle on the prairie to prevent their wandering too far from home. Two of us boys were assigned this task because one boy could not mount the horse alone. One boy was helped to the back of the horse. He in turn pulled the other one up so both could ride. Thus they rounded up the cattle and brought them home before sundown.

One day when we were watching the cattle, the sky became suddenly overcast. We were enveloped in a cloud of descending grasshoppers. They seemed to drop from the sky in uncounted millions and continued to come down in an endless stream. We helped each other on the horse, planning to round up the cattle and take them home. It was twilight because the sun had been darkened by the numerous grasshoppers. The horse turned his tail toward the storm and refused to move. We could not persuade him to go, so had to run home for father's help. When he came, he forced the horse to go with a whip.

When we reached home, mother had lighted a lamp in the house. She was in the garden trying to keep the grasshoppers from eating the vegetables. She had taken the clothesline and tied rags to it. She directed us to drag the rope over the garden. The grasshoppers, however, would fly up and then light again safely. So mother could only watch the garden disappear. The noise made by the millions of grasshoppers as they ate everything they could possibly devour was plainly heard.

Father took small bunches of hay on a pitchfork and lighted the hay with a match. He went among the nearest rows of corn. The blazing hay burned the wings of millions of grasshoppers. These insects furnished food for the chickens until spring came. Because of the grasshoppers, there was no grain to feed the chickens. Father took the hay made of wild grass into the straw stable and shook out the dead bodies of the grasshoppers. The chickens fed upon them, and it was the only food the chickens had during the long, cold winter.

This plague of grasshoppers appeared about three o'clock in the afternoon and before darkness fell over the land, not only the garden but the entire farm crop had been devoured. The grasshoppers were so numerous that every post, stick, and weed that offered a resting place for the night was occupied by these pests.

The plague of grasshoppers was general over northwest Iowa. Since the crops were destroyed, many of the homesteaders put their few belongings into a wagon and left their homestead. In the spring, those who stayed were forced to leave when they saw they would have to feed the millions of young grasshoppers.

The loss of their farm crop brought extreme hardship and

want to the homesteaders. In some counties the board of county supervisors tried to provide relief for the homesteaders that stayed, but so many demands were made, they could not raise enough money by taxation. A group was chosen to go back east to beg for food, clothing, and seed for the settlers. Our family was forced to leave in the spring of 1877. Father exchanged one eighty acres for a two-year-old steer which later sold for $15 and he exchanged the second eighty for a two-year-old heifer and a calf which he sold to a cattle buyer in Estherville for $12. So ended our homestead venture in what is now Clay County—ended for the sum of $27!

THE FUEL PROBLEM

At a very early date, coal mines about one mile north of Fort Dodge were opened. The grade of coal in them was inferior so they were later abandoned. The early homesteaders had great difficulty supporting their families through the long winters. During several of the winters a group of neighbors arranged with father to take their tools down to these mines in the fall. The men would remain at the mines until spring.

These trips to Fort Dodge and return sometimes took three or more weeks. One spring the roads were so bad that only the tools could be hauled in the wagon. The men walked all the way from Fort Dodge to their homesteads 12 miles northeast of Spencer.

On these long trips, father would stop in some sheltered place for the noon meal. There he could feed his team and eat a 5 cent loaf of bread and a ring of bologna. He would then start his long slow journey over the prairie again. If it was too cold to sleep under his wagon at night, he would get shelter in some homesteader's house.

At these coal mines the owners built crude barns for night shelter for the teams that took two or more days for the trip. The settler going for coal would put into his sled or wagon grain and hay enough for the trip and some food for himself. He would try to get his coal loaded the night he arrived at the mines. Then he would put his team into this barn, feed it, and try to find shelter for himself. There was a bunkhouse provided by the operator of the mines. There the homesteader could eat his frozen lunch, roll up in his horse blankets and try to sleep a few hours. He had no trouble awakening early so that he could feed his team, eat a few mouthfuls of lunch, and be well on the road before daylight.

Often on the main roads leading to the mines one could count more than thirty teams following close together, each loaded with coal going westward. Over these long prairie roads that wound in and out among the ponds, the drivers walked on the leeward side of the loads in order to keep from freezing. It was the custom of the early settlers to put a lamp in the window of their houses at night so that it might direct some belated homesteader to a place of safety.

Travel on these prairie roads was very lonely and uncertain. There were times when the homesteaders became so confused in the vast stretches of prairies, they had no idea where they were in the darkness. The early settlers were very hospitable and no traveler was ever turned away without first having his needs fulfilled.

PRAIRIE GRASS AND PRAIRIE FLOWERS

We boys who spent long hours on the prairies herding the cattle had many hours in which to explore the plants and wildlife we found there in great numbers. We were always so glad to see patches of black appear here and there when the warm days of spring came and the vast blanket of snow began to disappear slowly. The first flushes of green were seen along the lowlands and the borders of the ponds. On the hills that were most exposed to the sun and where the soil was poorest, the first spring flower appeared. It was the woolly calyxed pasque with its yellow center. It is sometimes called the windflower. As spring came on and the prairie grass appeared, almost at the same time one found the yellow upland buttercup. A little later on gopher knolls could be found the Johnny-jump-up or blue violet and an occasional downy yellow violet, the modest and retiring species of the violet family. These were succeeded by the less common bird's food violet with conspicuous blue. Then there followed in quick succession a great deal of color in flowers that seemed to battle with the prairie grass for a place. The grass produced such a heavy sod it was almost impossible for any other plant to get a hold. The little blue, purple, and white grass flowers that belong to the iris family were determined to get a foothold in the sod and they appeared. Then there was the yellow star grass; each flower a lovely five-pointed star on a slender stalk. This beautiful little flower belonged to the amaryllis family.

So the prairie became a wilderness of flowers which these

people had not seen in their eastern forested homes. There was the puccoon, the wild artichoke, wild indigo, spiderwort, wild garlic and onion, smartweed, butterfly weed or orange milkweed, bull thistle, wood betony or louswort, and the purple cone flower.

Later in the season the wild Sweet William appeared on the landscape. They were sure to be seen as they boldly lifted their heads above the grass that covered the uplands. They were the marvel of the prairie—pink, white, and purple—so fragrant that they perfumed the whole prairie atmosphere.

There was one upland lily—the queen of the prairie. The one who could bring home a handful of these prairie beauties kept the location a secret so that he could be the one with superior knowledge. Their flower stalks each bore a solitary red gem well above the grass; their five quivering anthers were poised upon the needle pointed filaments so that they might spill their brown pollen upon the club-shaped stigma. These lovely flowers have become extinct in Iowa.

The latter part of May and through June witnessed a profusion of wild roses—beautiful and fragrant. These roses may still be seen in Iowa along railroad right-of-ways and often along the highways protected from extinction by the shelter of the wire fence.

We hunted for the first flower stems of lady's tobacco which we chewed with much zest, not because it had any particular flavor but it colored the saliva and we could spit "tobacco juice"—a practice enjoyed by nearly every homesteader. Boys merely imitated their fathers with imitation tobacco juice though they were not quite as expert as the experienced tobacco chewer.

Then there was the oxalis or sorrel—two types. One was commonly called sheep sorrel; the other, wood sorrel. It had an exquisite purple flower with large leaves bearing brown coloring in them and supported by juicy stalks. Its juice was deliciously acid. Our stomachs had come through those long winters hungry for green things and this sorrel helped to satisfy that appetite.

With the coming of midsummer the yellows began to predominate. The tall rosin weed or compass plant, when it began to bloom, would have such an abundance of sap that it would break through the skin or bark and harden. Then the children would go from one stalk to another picking off this hardened sap to chew. We would have a quid of gum the equal of which was never sold at any shop. Along with this gum weed was to be found the black-eyed Susan. Several varieties of goldenrod were easily noticed. These continued to beautify the prairies until the frost came. Whenever the sod might be broken, such as at gopher knolls, there would be found a small type of wild sunflower.

The last prairie flowers to appear were several species of asters. These would continue to bloom until severely frozen.

Along with the slough grass that began to waken at the first touch of spring around the margin of ponds that had been burned the fall before, a few water plants began to appear. The iris or fleur-de-lis was attractive. The small-flowered lady's slipper, with exquisite odor, was much appreciated. Sometimes we were rewarded in our search by finding a yellow lady's slipper. The sagitaris, sweet flag, bulrush, cattail and sedge grass appeared in due time. With these water plants the muskrats were able to build their homes and from their roots and bulbs they obtained their food for the winter.

Someone who spent his boyhood with all these lovely wildflowers about him cannot but deeply regret their destruction and in many cases, complete extinction.

PRAIRIE SLOUGHS

One of the landmarks very familiar in old Iowa is now nearly all gone. That landmark was the prairie slough. Nothing slowed up the covered wagons as much nor made traveling so hard as the attempts that had to be made to cross the slough barriers. They were a terror to all travelers. At certain seasons of the year they seemed bottomless. It was a common experience to have to leave a wagon mired down to its axles.

In the early days there were no marked highways. One decided upon the general direction he wished to go and started toward it. Days might pass before he might meet another human being. No one ever passed another person going the same direction. So if anyone mired down or "sloughed down" as was the term used, he would have to find a way out by himself. No one ever went out on the prairie without a log chain or strong rope. It was a common experience for the driver to get out in the water and mud to tie this rope or hook the chain to the end of the tongue giving the team a better footing so they could pull their utmost. Often it was necessary to pry up the wheels. For this purpose a rail and something to use for blocking was carried. The pioneers often used oxen for teaming because they could wallow through the mud better.

Grass and wildflowers blanketed the seemingly limitless prairie when the Findlay boys were herding cattle near their home in northwest Iowa. From earliest spring until frost, the prairie presented an ever-changing panorama of color and vegetation. (PHOTO BY ROGER LANDERS)

——⦂⧁⦂⧂⧁⧃❮❯⧃⧂⧁⦂⧂⦂——

When our family came to Webster County in 1877 we drove two ox teams. We were compelled to "double up" several times a day. This meant we would put both teams on one wagon. One of the boys was given the task of driving the lead team through the almost impassable sloughs. That would mean he had to wade through the slough with the oxen. The other boy drove the ox team on the tongue. They would pull one wagon through and unfasten both teams of oxen. Then while one boy rode one of the oxen the other drove the teams back for the second wagon. They would then pull the second wagon up to solid ground. This occurred so often every day that the son who waded through removed his overalls and was dressed in only a hickory shirt. In that way he was prepared for any emergency. He didn't have to worry about coming upon other travelers unexpectedly and having them find him dressed in so few clothes. One could see for miles on the prairies and there were few travelers.

It often happened that when one of the wagons became mired down very badly, the movers would be compelled to carry the load to solid ground, pull the empty wagon from the mire, reload and go on to the next bottomless slough. It was not possible to go around these sloughs as one might imagine. There was a good inlet and outlet of water into them which could not be crossed at all in trying to go around. The only hope of crossing was to find a place where there were enough grass roots to make a solid tough sod that would support the wagon. But even then the wagon often broke through, sank to the axles and could not be moved. So the unloading process began. This unloading and reloading was often repeated so much that progress was slow and discouraging.

In the winter these prairie sloughs were frozen over—cold and dead as an iceberg. If they were deep enough so that they did not freeze to the bottom, they would be covered with muskrat houses. These houses were huge piles of coarse water plants and moss. Cattails and bulrushes were found in great quantity. The muskrats would remove all the plants from large areas, and the houses would be built around these open spaces. Small houses were feeding places where the rats would carry the roots and water plants under the ice to these houses to feed upon. The large houses were well built and space provided with room for several rats at one time. These rooms were above the water level and provided with soft, dry moss for bedding.

Trapping was the only way to obtain a living during the winter months. One fall father made us a small boat so we could "pole" around from one rat house to another for fall trapping. Rats feed at night and they would eat on the outside of the house until the ice formed and the rats were forced inside. During the fall we set traps on the outside of the house. There was only one place on the house where the muskrats would climb out of the water. At that place there was an easy grade from the edge of the water to the top of the house. There, at the edge of the water we would set our traps. When we could get on the ice, we would cut into the houses with an ax and set the traps where the rats came in to feed or sleep. We learned from experience how to best approach and cut into these houses. To successfully open one of these houses, it was necessary to make the opening opposite the entrance the rats used. Then the trap could be set at the water's edge and skillfully covered. Then the opening was as skillfully closed. If the opening was carelessly closed, the house would freeze up and the trap be frozen into the ice. If that happened it would take much time and hard labor to remove the house in order to get to the trap and cut it out of the ice. Much work would be done needlessly and still no rats caught. If the rats found the hole carelessly closed, they would sometimes carry moss and completely fill the house, and the trap would be buried in the material brought in by the rats.

The rat pelts were sold to fur buyers who came to the homes of settlers. Sometimes we would send them to Spencer or Milford where they would get a cent or two more for each pelt. The price in those days was 10 cents each for muskrat pelts. If we were fortunate enough to get 12½ cents each, we felt very lucky. Occasionally we caught a mink, and that would bring a big price. For an extra fine mink pelt, we would sometimes get $5.00, but the usual price was $2.50.

In the summertime these sloughs were the homes of a great variety of bird life: geese, ducks, loons, mud hens, bitterns or "shitepokes," and gulls. Blackbirds nested among the reeds and on the old muskrat houses. The rats never fussed over the birds using their homes, because in the summer the rats are a lazy lot. When winter approached, the rats began to build but they never rebuilt an old house.

Several kinds of small mollusks, coiled shells, made their homes in these fresh waters. These mollusks lived and died in these prairie sloughs for countless ages. When a prairie fire would sweep through these sloughs in the fall, these mollusks were killed by the heat. Then the winds would blow these empty and bleached shells together in great quantities, so that at a distance these beds of shells often looked like piles of white gravel.

PRAIRIE FIRES

In the early days in northwest Iowa when there were miles upon miles of prairie covered with dry grass, nothing could stop the prairie fires that would sweep over those grass plains with the speed of a racehorse. It was very dangerous to be caught in the path of such a fire. There was one way of safety, if there was time. By starting a fire near the place to be protected and then whipping it out on one side and allowing the other side to run where it would, a safety zone was provided. In this way a controlled fire could be led along near the hay stables, sodhouse, haystacks and the small fields of grain, thus saving them. The early settlers called this "back-firing." It was their only sure protection. Plowing a strip around one's buildings did not always insure the property against loss.

After the frost had killed the vegetation and it became dry, every homesteader was worried about the danger of prairie fires. During that season no homesteader ever went to bed without first going outside the house and scanning the horizon on every side for any signs of fire.

One fall night father came in after scanning the horizon and said, "The sky is lighted far to the north, and I fear a prairie fire since the wind is blowing from the northeast." We went to bed but some time during the night, father awakened us. In a minute we were dressed and outside. As far as the eye could see east and west, there was an oncoming wall of fire that made everything as easy to see as if it were day.

With the usual foreplanning of the homesteader, father had pumped the trough full of water when he had finished the evening chores. He had pails at the well ready for an emergency. North of the buildings and haystack was a large slough. Between the slough and the buildings father had plowed a strip at least 20 rods in width as a fireguard. He had done this early in the fall. In an instant, each member of the family was set at his particular job. Father handled the buckets. On came this wall of fire which enveloped the slough with its dry growth of grass, reeds and cattails. The terrible flames leaped many feet into the air. This caused a draught that urged the flames to take long jumps when the draught would suddenly whip the top or crest of these awful billows of flame down to the ground. Thus the flame would sometimes ignite the grass many feet ahead of the wall of fire that licked up everything that would burn.

Even across the 20-rod strip of plowing, the heat was almost unbearable. The abandoned nests of mice and birds, all ablaze, came rolling across this plowed strip driven by the wind created in the burning swamp. We thought of the ball nests as demons who wanted to destroy everything the homesteaders had. It was the children's job to stop these balls of fire and extinguish them with sacks dipped into the pails of water that their father brought to them. In a very short time the danger was past. That night many a poor homesteader lost everything he had.

This fire had started near Spirit Lake and covered many square miles of area. It swept on toward Spencer where it seriously threatened to burn that small town. It went on south of Spencer. The homesteaders often wondered what brought these fires to an end. The prairies went on and on.

If there was any vegetation that escaped the fall prairie fires, someone was sure to light it the next spring. But the spring fires did not burn so vigorously as the fall ones did. It was a thrilling sight for us as we watched on dark nights. We saw the different lines of fire moving across the level ground. They looked like pictures we had seen of companies and regiments in an army. The tall slough grass burned rapidly; others burned slower, and so the lines of fire became irregular—armies in battle array.

After the prairies had been burned over by the spring fires, flocks of thousands of pigeons could be seen feeding on what they found of insects and seeds left on the ground after the fire. They were beautiful birds, dark-colored with gold or yellowish brown breasts. Occasionally father would shoot a mess of these pigeons for a meal. They were never known to the homesteaders by any other name than "prairie pigeons."

If the spring fires occurred late enough, the boys would go out after one of them with a pail to pick up prairie chickens' eggs. They would get a pailful in a short time. These prairie hens liked the dry grass in which to build their nests. The fire would burn the nests and leave the white eggs showing a long distance against the blackened prairie. The eggs were not hurt by the fire and if they were fresh, they could be eaten.

The early settlers were very careless about birdlife. No one ever thought that the time would ever come when wild birds and fowls would be scarce and in some cases gone altogether. It seemed then that the supply would last forever and no one ever thought of protecting or conserving them. Along with the passing of these wild birds have passed the prairies and so the prairie fires. Very early in Iowa laws were made to punish persons who purposely or carelessly caused prairie fires.

HOME REMEDIES

When we left Illinois to come to Iowa in 1870, mother anticipated some of the hardships to which the homesteader would be subjected. So she collected many of the home remedies consisting of medicines, herbs, and ordinary drugs. Our homestead was 15 miles from the nearest doctor. These 15 miles of trackless prairie deepened mother's anxiety.

When one of us had a stomachache, there was the peppermint, a few drops of it in a little sweetened water. If the pain was severe and kept on for a long time, the peppermint treatment would be followed by a dose of pain killer or "hot drops" as it was sometimes called. We dreaded that dose of pain killer. We would try hard to avoid showing any pain in order to escape it.

When one had a cold, mother often made a syrup of stewed onions in sugar. A spoonful of that was given all too often, the children thought. When the cold was bad and would not break up, the chest was treated with a mixture of kerosene, turpentine, and goose grease or skunk's oil. This mixture was thoroughly rubbed in. Then the chest was covered with a soft flannel. If the throat was sore, mother prepared several gargles. The gargle to be used depended upon the degree of soreness. These gargles ranged between weak salt water, used hot, and a gargle composed of hot water, black pepper, vinegar, and salt. This latter gargle was accompanied by wrapping the neck with a woolen stocking that could not be taken off until the throat was completely well.

Another remedy used to help get rid of a bad cold was a drink of hot ginger tea. The reason this was given was that it was supposed to warm up the inside organs. Anyone who ever took hot ginger was sure the remedy worked because his "insides" felt as if they were being burned by an internal fire.

Medicines to prevent sickness were used in those days, too. When we were small, we wore asafetida bags hung around our necks to ward off diseases that were said to be "catching." This was before the germ idea was well understood. There was another preventive method which we dreaded. If there was any danger of our taking some disease that was known to be in the neighborhood, mother brought out a bottle containing some small, home-grown red peppers covered with vinegar. A tablespoon of this medicine was the regulation dose. Mother called this "pepper sauce," but that was really a mild way to express it. When we had once swallowed it, we had no trouble knowing just where it was on the inside.

The tonic we took in the spring was not one suggested by a doctor and made up in the drugstore. Occasionally we did buy a few drugs such as sassafras, wahoo, and aloes at the drugstore. These were mixed with poplar bark, wild cherry bark, white ash bark, prickly ash bark and bloodroot which we were able to collect in the neighborhood. These were all cut into small pieces and pounded together. These were all put into a large-necked bottle and covered with whiskey. This was allowed to stand for a few days. The dose was one tablespoon before breakfast.

Then there were the herbs that were gathered, dried, and preserved for emergencies—that is, for the day when an ounce of prevention might be worth a pound of cure. Boneset, mullein, pennyroyal, horsemint, smartweed, sage, and catnip were a few of the most common ones.

When anyone sprained a joint, it was wrapped in a cloth saturated in vinegar and salt. If it was a severe sprain, an application of beef gall dissolved in vinegar was applied to the injury. The gall bladder of the beef butchered on the farm was saved, dried, and preserved for such emergencies. If one had a boil, a poultice of soft soap and brown sugar was put on it. A similar poultice or a slice of salt pork was bound to a wound to "draw out" the poison or to bring it to a "head."

Mother sniffed at many of the cures recommended by some of the pioneer neighbors. Every remedy she used and every cure she applied had to be a tried one that met commonsense and had properly cured someone.

THE WELL ON THE OLD FARM

When we bought the forty acres in Otho Township in 1877, there was no well on the place that furnished water fit for use in the home. For many years we carried all the water used for drinking and cooking from the farmhouse across the road.

In the early eighties this section of Iowa had a long period of drought. All of the shallow wells failed and we were without water. It kept us busy hauling water from the river for the livestock that could not be driven down to the river.

It was then that I suggested to father that we try to dig a well where water had been located by the "witches." Father marked off a circle 3½ feet in diameter. The center was the point marked by the "water witches." The spot had been marked by a steel drag tooth driven into the ground. The digging started.

We built a tripod with some poles. We put ropes and pulleys on it. Then we pulled out the dirt with a horse.

After a while the air down in the hole became very bad so we had to change more often. We dug the well to a depth of 47 feet.

Father scolded to think we had taken such a risk in bad air. He would allow neither of us to go down again. He was determined to have the hole filled up again and try to get a well at some other location.

In a few days after we had begged him not to make us give up the well, he tested it again. That day the air was better and the lantern would burn to the bottom of the well. That proved it was safe to work in.

We had a 2-inch auger which we had welded to a steel pole 10 feet long. We begged father to let us bore down the length of the auger while he was at home to help. Then, if there was no sign of water, we would give up the job. The bucket to receive the dirt and the auger were taken to the bottom of the well. Above the head of the boy in the well hung a hook attached to a rope which the horse would pull out of the well with the attached bucket of dirt at a given signal. He had bored almost the full length of the auger when water began to seep out of the hole around the auger. He called to the top of the well that he had found water. He became very excited, fearing that he might not get out. He called for us to hurry.

When we hurriedly hoisted him to the top, we sat there wondering if the water might not run over the top because it was coming in so fast. When it finally came to a stop, it was 10 feet from the top of the hole. It is now over fifty years since the well was built but the water has not lowered enough to be noticed.

WILDLIFE ADVENTURES

When we homesteaded in Clay County, the wild game was abundant.

Father was an excellent shot and kept the two families supplied with meat, using his twelve gauge, double-barreled, muzzle-loading shotgun.

The sand-hill cranes would come to the small field of corn after it was planted in such numbers that one of the boys had to be responsible for scaring them away. We liked to watch the cranes and their antics. They would run and jump and scream. Father only shot but one which mother tried in vain to cook so that it could be eaten. Father was a true sportsman. Game was very abundant, but he never shot a bird or animal except for food or its pelt.

Every season father shot dozens of geese, hundreds of prairie chickens, many ducks, and occasionally a brant. Sometimes he would shoot a mess of plovers, and once in the spring, he shot a mess of wild pigeons. We never liked the flavor of the curlew and the snipe because they always tasted of snails. One can hardly believe that wildlife was once so abundant.

After we came to Webster County, the wild waterfowl was so abundant everybody could have all the wild meat they could consume. We always left some corn standing in the shocks until we needed it during the winter. The prairie chickens would come by the thousands when the snow covered their food. They would alight among these shocks of corn. We would make a trap of laths with doors in the top that would open downward. We would suspend ears of corn above these doors and the prairie chickens were attracted to the top of the trap. When a chicken would step upon the door, it would tip down and drop the chicken inside the cage. Then the door would go back to its original position ready for another hungry and innocent prairie chicken. We sometimes went out to these traps with sacks and found we had caught from twenty to thirty of these chickens at one time—as many as we could carry. In those days there was no closed season on game of any kind.

Fish were abundant in the streams and lakes of northern Iowa. There were no fish laws for the homesteader to observe.

Probably that was a good idea because the pioneer got much of his food by hunting and fishing. Flesh food made up much of the early settler's diet.

The inlet to Trumbull Lake ran across one corner of our homestead. All we had to do was to go to this small stream, cast a hook, and in a few minutes the family would be provided with a mess of pickerel.

This sod-bound inlet into the lake was a very peculiar stream. In some places the kind of soil and the knotted roots of the tall slough grass kept the water from widening the stream. Then suddenly the inlet would burst into a broad, deep hole, deep enough to easily swim a horse. These holes were found where there was less grass to hold the soil. In these holes an abundance of fish could be found at all times of the year.

Usually in the latter part of April or in the early days in May, the buffalo fish would start "running" or would migrate from the large bodies of water such as the lakes and go out into the streams to spawn. When any settler found out that the buffalo were "running," it was expected that he would tell the other settlers. This "run" lasted but a few days. Farmers would hitch up their ox teams and trudge away armed with a spear. If they were too poor to own a spear, they would bring a pitchfork. It is hard to believe that a homesteader would get a wagon box of buffalo in a few hours by standing on the bank of these small streams and spearing the buffalo as they passed. They didn't have to quarrel about the best place to stand. There were plenty of buffalo passing the last man on the bank. There was a mill pond at old Milford below the old Arnold Mill to which many homesteaders would go. The buffalo would go through the outlet of the mill pond in such numbers that the mill was closed down. These fish were thrown out on the banks with the spear or pitchfork until the homesteader was tired. Then he would select from them the ones he wanted, enough to fill his wagon box if he wanted that many, and start home. When he reached home, the whole family would be engaged in cleaning fish. Some would be salted and some would be smoked for the use of the family in the summer. No one then ever thought that such slaughter of fish might some day exhaust the supply.

I BEAT IT OUT
TO THE BLACK HILLS

Bruce Siberts

EACH PART AND PARCEL *of the great expanse between the oceans played its historic part as pioneers moved relentlessly across the continent and put together something called America. But no other section of the country so captured the imagination and so fascinated people, even in other countries, as the saga of "the West."*

It had everything: limitless expanses of prairie and sky, tribal Indians, danger, hardship, remoteness, lawlessness, cattle, horses, guns, the harshest kind of weather, death. Its demands on human beings were without parallel short of war. And there was some of that.

The romance of "the West" has been recorded in history without end: in fiction, and in movies that are an industry in themselves. But just good, authentic, first-person, I-was-there recitals of what human beings (primarily men) went through as they rode out across the upper great plains for the first time are few in number.

A fortunate, five-year effort at collaboration between one of those clearly in a position to "tell it like it was" and a well-known author and thoroughgoing professional in the area of history has recorded one of the fine first-person histories of the upper great plains.

Bruce Siberts was a twenty-two year old Iowa boy when he headed for South Dakota in 1890. For fifteen years he lived some of this nation's most romantic history (although much of it was anything but romantic) and saw it unfold there before his eyes. He had a story to tell. Fortunately, fate brought him together with an author and historian who spent five years organizing and editing many thousands of pages of Siberts's handwritten notes.

The result, one of the truly fine pieces of literature of the West, was published by the University of Oklahoma Press which has granted permission to reprint the photographs and the following excerpts from the book, Nothing but Prairie and Sky: Life on the Dakota Range in the Early Days.

Bruce Siberts is deceased but the man to whom all readers are indebted for organizing and editing his recollections—and giving them literary value—is Dr. Walker D. Wyman, Centennial Year Distinguished Professor of History, Wisconsin

State University—River Falls. Dr. Wyman is the author of several other books and was president of University of Wisconsin—Whitewater.

———꧁꧂———

T the age of twenty-two, I beat it out to the Black Hills to make my fortune, worked around for a year or two, and finally became a cattle and horse rancher myself. The range country west of the Missouri didn't have much in it but prairie and sky and livestock in the sixteen years I was there, but I got along pretty well. I drank enough alkali water to rust my pipes, made some money raising horses, got into a number of scrapes, and all in all, got pretty well acquainted with what pioneer life was like on the last American frontier.

It was on the evening of July 8, 1890, that I climbed on a baggage car at Mount Pleasant, Iowa, and started out.

I got to Hill City, a little Black Hills settlement that like all the others called itself a city and hoped to be the center of the universe within a few years. I got a place at a boarding camp one night and the next stayed in the barn at a small mine. The boss and his wife were nice people. They had five men working for them, had found some good ore and some tin, but they were nearly out of money. The woman had a little organ, and she played and sang for us that night. When I started on north the next morning, she told me I would be better off if I went back to Iowa. At Deadwood City, where meals were about a dollar, I bought a can of cherries and a loaf of bread for my dinner, and as I ate it, I wondered if the woman wasn't right.

Pierre was a lively place in 1890. It had a population of six or seven thousand, and the speculators had laid out additions 5 or 6 miles from town. Both Pierre and Fort Pierre across the river were trading points for the Sioux, and a lot of them were coming and going all the time. Many of them were trying to get hold of the forty-four Winchester repeating rifles, model 1873. There was some talk of an outbreak of the Sioux, who were surly and hateful. Some of the white people remembered the Sioux trouble following the Custer massacre and told stories of the killing and torture at that time.

In the 5,000-square-mile area, bounded on the south by the Black Hills–Pierre trail, on the east by the Missouri, and on the north and west by the Cheyenne, were no more than forty whites. And one of them was trying to claim most of the country. Iowa was never like this.

The cattle business looked like a good one to me in 1891. It figured good on paper. Borrow money at 10 percent, buy a few cows, and the herd will double every three years. Start with 100, three years later you have 200, then 400, 800, 1,600, 3,200, 6,400, and so on. There was lots of grass in that 11,000,000-acre pasture taken from the Sioux in 1889, and there were very few settlers. Of course, it was a hard life, with cold winters and hot summers, alkali water, and danger of Indian uprisings, but it looked mighty good to me.

I took up a claim on Plum Creek where there was a good spring. I bought a five-dollar cabin that was on it. The Indians seemed to have given up the idea of Ghost Dancing and war and were moving back to their camps, rounding up their cattle, and settling down again. They still had to go to Fort Bennett once a month to draw beef and flour. This kept them on the road a good deal of the time. Some of the young men were being doctored the Indian way for their wounds received at the Battle of Wounded Knee, that is, by keeping the wounds open. It looked wrong to me, but I found out later that it worked. Anyway, they were now a defeated people and lived under the control of Uncle Sam's army and their own blue-uniformed policemen, who rode around a lot with their revolvers showing.

The white ranchers were an average lot of people in most ways. They had to stand a lot of hardships such as droughts and blizzards. But all of them added to their herds by branding slicks. It was not considered stealing if one put his brand on young stock that were not following or suckling their mothers. Most people

Bruce Siberts, twenty-one in this photograph, was only twenty-two when he migrated to South Dakota in 1890. As a rancher, he found it took a hardy man to cope with the demands of that sparsely populated state. He learned to be as tough as the next man and to hold his own whether on the open range or in the settlements.

never bothered to eat their own beef. Since the bigger outfits swept away a lot of stock belonging to the little men at roundup time, it was proper for the little men to eat beef that carried a big outfit's brand.

I always got along well with the Indians who lived across the Cheyenne River. They were a lot better than some of the white men I got to know. If you went to their camps hungry, they would feed you their best jerked beef, bread, and coffee. Their style of eating was crude in manners but skillful in operation. With a knife they dug out a piece of meat, stuck one end in their mouth, cut off a good mouthful, then whetted the knife on the sole of a moccasin. If they got grease on their fingers, they rubbed it in their hair. The cutting of the meat looked dangerous as the knife came close to their long noses.

The women were patient workers but not good looking. At fifteen to twenty they were handsome, but they faded fast and soon became shapeless. Most of them were virtuous. Prostitutes were marked with a gunpowder tattoo dot in the middle of the forehead. The young girls were kept neat and clean and did very little work. The women cut and carried the wood, while the bucks hunted some, but mostly took it easy. The Indians had their good points all right.

The winter of 1890–1891 was a tough one for both whites and Indians in Dakota. I had only cotton underwear and no way to get any woolens. I did trade for a big buffalo coat and got hold of a blue-gray army coat and a pair of cavalry boots. The boots were all right in the fall and spring, but in the winter one needed German knit sox, felt boots, and overshoes, none of which I had that first year. When the temperatures got down below zero, the Indians wrapped their feet in jack-rabbit skins and then put on moccasins. They refused to wear the U.S. Issue shoes as they were nearly all too big and heavy for them. We could buy all these shoes from them we wanted at 15 cents a pair. I.D. Issue coats for 25 cents, and blankets for $1. My house was cold, but after I got my buffalo coat I could at least sleep without freezing at night.

My claim was a lonesome place until I got used to it, being about 20 miles from the nearest rancher. Cavanaugh and Cheyenne City were the same distance to the northwest. Pierre was 90 miles one way, and the Sioux camps were strung across the Cheyenne River.

My claim was nothing but a piece of prairie when I moved

out there with my wagon, my two ponies, a stove, and a few pots and pans.

I had bought a cabin from old Circle Lame and decided to move it. It took me about a day to take the cabin apart and move it and about a week to put it together again. Hay had to be cut to lay on top the roof poles, and dirt had to be thrown on top of them. I used an old pail for a stovepipe hole and chinked the logs with homemade mud. I didn't bother with a floor. From the Robinson store I got enough boxes for chairs and tables. This was the first house I ever owned, and I was pretty proud of it.

In my first winter on the Dakota prairie I learned how to camp out in the wintertime. When I was working for the Robinsons and after I got out on my own, we made trips about twice a month to Pierre for goods. It was quite a job to keep from freezing on these trips of 90 miles. Walking along by the side of the wagon, picking up wood and cowchips for fuel, was about the only way, even though we had buffalo coats and blankets. At night we camped in a sheltered place among the ash groves, picketed the horses, and slept on the ground around a fire that we tried to keep going all night. Sometimes we could kill a little fresh meat along the way.

These trips were tough on our noses, cheeks, and fingers. Oftentimes, they would burn and itch when we got into a warm room. Looking back on these trips, I wonder how we fared so well.

Pierre was a welcome sight when we came in off the frozen prairie. We headed for a livery stable where we put the team and then checked in at a hotel. A lot of cattlemen spent their winters in town, and they, with the soldiers coming and going to the Dakota forts, made business lively. It was booming in 1890–1891. Horse-drawn streetcars ran up the hill to East Pierre where a big promoter had built the Wells House. The busiest place was the red-light district. It was always crowded with freighters, soldiers, and a lot of halfbreeds. Only one or two houses catered to full-blooded Sioux. Every saloon sold a lot of bad whiskey and Sioux Falls beer, and tin horn gamblers kept the faro and poker tables busy. In fact, saloons, livery stables, and the red-light district made up the biggest part of the business of the town.

It wasn't easy to leave the politicians, the pimps, and the pretty girls of Pierre and go back to my dirt-floored, 8 by 16 shack on Plum Creek and live on my own cooking and with my own company most of the time. But once back to what a man called home, it wasn't a bad place to be. Now and then in the evenings, I would hum to myself "Golden Slippers" or "Dan McGinty."

☆   ☆   ☆

[*"After a dull summer of putting up hay,"* as Siberts put it, he *decided to buy some cattle "and see if they would use the multiplication tables for me." To buy the cattle he went to O'Neill, Nebraska.*]

At noon the next day I was in the Irish settlement [O'Neill, Nebraska] named after the Fenian, John O'Neill. It was a wide-open town and pretty rough. The settlers were hard up, but the Wyoming cowboys and gamblers kept the red-light district and the saloons booming. I went to the Star Livery Barn where I bought twenty cows and six calves, paying $400 which I had borrowed, and set out for the William Griffiths', old family friends, who lived north of there 20 miles.

At the Niobrara the steers balked and acted like they had never seen water before. Four Indian boys rode their ponies across to help me. I led a gentle cow across and her calf followed. The boys drove the rest over and we all got across in good shape. When I gave the Indians two sacks of Bull Durham and papers for cigarets, they were so pleased they went along with me for 4 or 5 miles. At noon that day I stopped at a wild plum patch and ate a lot of them. That night I penned my cattle at Spencer, a new town of shacks and small stores, and slept in the hotel. I spent the next night with an old homesteader who had more than his share of bedbugs. This was the last of the partly settled country. I followed an old Indian trail northwest through a good grass country and got to Bonesteel where I spent the night with Jack Sully, who had been in the country for years. He had an Indian wife, a son, and a hired man, and was putting up hay for winter feed when I ran across him. I found him very pleasant and intelligent, and he refused to take any pay for my staying with him. We ate beef that night, but not from his herd.

Until I got to White River the next evening, I never saw a soul. A family of full bloods lived there, had a garden and a corn-field and a small herd of cattle and ponies. For my food and lodging the man said I could give the woman 25 cents as she wanted to buy a comb. A quarter and two sacks of tobacco pleased them very much. After crossing the river, I followed the Chamber-

Sioux Indians en route to Fort Bennett for rations, about 1899.

⟶ ⟶⟩⟨⟩⟨ ⟩⟨⟩⟨⟩⟨ ⟨⟵

lain–Black Hills trail and met two ox-teams of German Mennon-nites, or Russians as they were called, going east to Chamberlain, which was the end of the Milwaukee Railroad at that time. One talked English and told me they had a colony on Medicine Creek 25 miles northwest.

Here I was at the Medicine Creek Russian colony 60 miles from Pierre and 150 miles from my log mansion on Plum Creek. There were no ranches between the settlements, and I had a badly spoiled, unbroken mare and 26 big and little cattle worth $400. Being my first venture, these cows seemed to me as valuable as all the gold in the Black Hills. From one of the Russians I got two loaves of bread and a dozen hard-boiled eggs for a quarter and started out. The mare did not want to leave her old haunts and would rear and fall back, so I had to lead her or risk being killed or crippled out in this no-man's-land. In the first two days I ate the bread and eggs, and the next day I lived on plums. Fort Pierre looked good to me that afternoon at four.

Going from Pierre to Plum Creek, I got tired of sardines and tomatoes but had no trouble with the cattle. The first night I stayed at a road ranch, the only one on the way home. The bed looked fair but was so full of bedbugs that I finally went out to the barn and slept on the hay. After that I slept on buffalo grass and covered myself with an old comfort. At Robinson's store I got some grub and pushed on home. I found everything all right in the cabin, but cattle had pretty well cleaned up the feed outside. The next day I raided the Indian preacher's garden on the big flat and got a sack full of corn and potatoes. I was now ready to settle down to the life of a rancher and watch the herd grow. One can pass away a good many hours by just watching the calves play and the cows fill themselves with grass.

☆   ☆   ☆

One day in January, 1892, I rode to the Deep Creek breaks where my cattle ranged and found nothing but a lot of empty space and a dim trail leading southwest left by the hooves of my cows and a couple of horses. With tears in my eyes and a Colt in my hand, I followed the trail for 20 miles or so before coming home with a tired horse.

There was more than cattle at stake, so I rigged up a bedroll and a cook outfit and started toward the Bad Lands. In a couple of days I went through Cedar Pass on the old Indian trail and found a campsite off the road. There was a seep of water from a spring for my horses to drink, but I had to melt snow for my coffee. Sage hens and rabbits were plentiful so I had meat to eat.

This country had been called Bad Lands by the Indians, and the whites had counted it no good. It seemed desolate and lonely as I started to look over the place. There were a lot of old camps, mostly Indian, with rusty cans and other junk around. Bones were all over. Buffalo horns were old and ready to go back to nothing. Elk horns were still solid. Small herds of antelope and mountain sheep, all pretty shy, were around. Coyotes and big, gray, lobo wolves were all over. Cattle and horses were plentiful in most places. Some of the horses had saddle and harness marks on them. Most of all, there was just lots of scenery, a kind of a jungle of land, and one could get lost easy if you did not spot trails and landmarks as you went along.

After roaming around there for a week, I gave up my cattle as lost and headed back. I still had hope of finding some of them in the spring roundups, but I had a better idea as to how to get back into the cattle business again.

I had made up my mind. My 31 cattle were gone. There was no workable law to protect me in my losses. Though I was scared of the deal, I had decided to get even. Fleming [a neighbor] and I bought a light wagon from the Indians, U.S. Issue not to be sold, and rigged up a small mess box with cooking kettles, dutch oven, bedding, and ropes. Fleming threw in his old Winchester for good measure.

One February day we started out, wrapped up in buffalo coats and felt boots and trailed by our two saddle horses.

We bought a lot of grub, including a four-dollar gallon jug of whiskey, and struck out for the Bad Lands the next morning in zero weather. Two and one-half days later, after chopping through 16-inch ice to water the horses and nearly freezing on the open prairie, we were in the center of the Bad Lands.

For two days we scouted around this strange country. There were deep creeks and draws impossible to cross, and mountains and hills so rough that a horse couldn't get over them. The horses we found were pretty snorty at first, but we got them to camp all right. While we were there, we rode them a lot to save ours. We found one bunch of sixteen tame gray horses with no brands on them, led by an old white mare with harness marks on her. There was one full-grown stallion in the bunch, but he didn't cause any trouble. We drove them into the canyon, made a rough catch pen out of ash poles fastened to trees, and put a dim brand on their left hips.

Fleming and I caught some of our slicks [unbranded range animals] and trimmed their manes and tails which made them look more like farm stock. We sold all the new ones except the old mare for $40 apiece, and were paid on the spot in five-, ten-, and twenty-dollar gold pieces. By spending two weeks and around $50 for supplies, we had made $600. I hadn't quite recovered my $400 loss on cows, but I had made a good beginning.

☆   ☆   ☆

It takes a tough man to stand the work of a roundup. The hands are up at daybreak and have breakfast before it really gets light. Everyone rolls his own tarpaulin, quilts, and blankets into a tight roll and loads it on the bed wagon. The cook and volunteer help wash the dishes while the four horses used on the bed wagon and the four for the chuck wagon are brought around and harnessed. The riders saddle up and some start taking the rough edges off their broncs, which have to do some unlimbering every morning before settling down for the day. The cook climbs on his wagon, the nighthawk on the bed wagon, and the day wrangler gathers his stock at the rear. The boss details one man to pilot the outfit on to the next campground. The boss does not get on his horse until the wagons are on the move and likely does not say a word. When he gets on, that is the signal that the riding has started for the day. The cowhands follow the boss to a hill on a stiff lope, and he sends ten men this way, six that way, and so on. He has to know his country well or he would lose the outfit every day. While the boss makes his way with the wagons and loose stock to the next camp 8 or 10 miles away, the circle riders begin their sweeps. All will meet by night at the next camp where the sorting of the different brands takes place.

After the pilot gets his outfit to the campground, one wrangler keeps the horses away from the cook's water hole. The pilot and the other wrangler then unharness the horses, leaving the collars, harness, and bridles where the wagons stopped. Two of them start on a lope to find some dry wood while the cook begins his fire with what little wood he has in the wagon. In a pretty good time the men are back, dragging wood at the end of their ropes. It is everybody's job to keep the water buckets filled, plenty of wood handy, and help the cook wash dishes, as he is a very busy man getting meals for fifty men or more. There is meat to cook, bread to make, dried fruit to soak, beans to bake, and other things to fix that taste awful good to hungry men. If the cook wants beef, he orders it, and they pick out a fat two- or three-year-old heifer, shoot her near the wagon, butcher her on the hide, and hang up to cure what is not cooked fresh.

Before the boss and some of the riders come in with some of the cattle, the pilot and the wranglers have made a rope corral for the saddle stock at some distance from the chuck wagon so the dust will not blow on the food. The space for 50 feet around the cook is holy ground and the cook is the Almighty. If things go wrong, he will raise hell. Maybe he will anyway. He is the only one who can cuss not only the hands but the boss, too.

All this time the day herders are bringing the herd along slowlike behind the saddle horses. These cattle are the ones being moved to another range and are herded day and night. Day herders go on duty as soon as they eat breakfast, and it is a tedious, poky job but easier than riding the long circle. Some days they may not move, and the herders can sit in the saddle on a little knoll and take it easy. One may take a nap while the others ride around the herd. While the bunch is bedded down at night, they take a two-hour turn every other night. Day herding was not a popular job.

A herd of beef near Fort Pierre.

☆   ☆   ☆

It's an ill wind that blows nobody good. Maybe, if my cattle had never been stolen by those outlaws, it might have taken me years to plunge in deep enough to buy over 100 head at a crack. Maybe, if I had not gone to the Bad Lands with Fleming, I might not have been around him when he sold his herd. Anyway, I was in the cattle business in 1892, and already I had learned that there was more to it than turning cattle loose on government land while I sat back and watched them double in number every year.

I was getting low on cash and in need of a few things, so I decided to ship twenty of my critters. After three days spent looking at the back end of a cow, I penned them in Pierre, ordered feed for them, and went to a restaurant for a good meal. The next day I cleaned up some and bought some new clothes with my fifty-dollar advance. Later I got a draft for the first stock I ever sold. They averaged 1,090 pounds in Chicago, and after the freight and commission were taken out, I had $560. That price wouldn't let anyone get rich very fast, but it was a mighty comforting feeling to have some cash in my pockets for the first time.

When I got tired of cutting ash and cedar posts that winter, and that was pretty often, I visited around quite a bit where I could pick up a meal or two and talk to someone. One of the most interesting trips that I made several times was up to the Cherry Creek subagency to see the Indians get their monthly ration issue from the government. On ration day all the Indians in that neck of the woods moved in on the agency with their dogs and ponies, and it was quite a show.

I suppose life was pretty dull for most of these Indians, and the trip after food was a big event. They started gathering about a week before the issue day and spent their time gambling, horse-racing, and just visiting. There were always a few half-civilized white men there to sell liquor to these wild savages in spite of the law against it. Most of these people were hungry, having nothing left but flour, and some of them didn't have that. On the big day, the Indian police climbed into the corrals with their big revolvers and began killing the sixty or seventy Texas steers inside. They shot them through the heart from the side, not in the head as white men do. When they got the cattle down, the boss farmer divided them and teams dragged the carcasses out to the various villages. Then the women took over and did the butchering. In about an hour everybody was eating fresh beef and cooking more. This went on all day and most of the night.

☆　　　☆　　　☆

Before the South Dakota winter closed in on us, it was the practice to go into Pierre and get enough grub to last most of the winter. I did this in October and dug a hole in my cabin's dirt floor and put the stuff in it. An old quilt covered it. As long as one was around and had a fire, it didn't freeze. We made no sheds for the livestock but did put up some haystacks to help get them through the winter.

I had a yen to go back to the Bad Lands to get some more horses but did not want to go alone. I decided to go anyway, so got my camping stuff together and started.

It was no trouble to find the place where Fleming and I had camped the winter before. A pile of our firewood and an old ax were still there. I chopped a hole in the ice to water my two horses and made a cold camp. The next morning I took my slowest horse to look around. There were a lot of Missouri John's horses scattered all over. I found one bunch of slicks that had two nice yearlings in it, and the next day I got on my sorrel mare and tried to chase them into my trap there in the bend where I had my camp. They drove easy until I got within a mile of the place, then a little white mare with red ears turned off on a ridge and led the bunch in some broken country. I wound up 10 miles from camp with a played-out horse. The mare staggered and acted like she would fall. She would hold her head down, shake it, and scatter sweat all over me. I let her drink, but the alkali water only made her feel worse. I was ashamed for having run a good horse this way when there wasn't a chance. It takes an awful good horse carrying a rider to outrun a wild bunch. So I made up my mind to quit and go home. I walked all the way back to camp, picketed the two horses, and cooked some coffee, bacon, and flapjacks before I went to bed. I knew the project had failed.

When I woke up and looked for my horses the next morning, they were gone. The ropes had been cut, and there were tracks of a man and a horse in the snow. I got breakfast quick and started on the trail but never saw hide nor hair of them. When I got back cold and tired, someone had been there and burned my saddle and bed. Here I was afoot 100 miles from home and the world looked pretty blue. If I hadn't stored some of my grub and an extra U.S. blanket in a little cave, I would have frozen to death that night. But I curled up in that cave and found myself alive in the morning.

The next morning I moved my camp to a little pocket about a mile toward White River. It had a washout cave so I could be a little more protected. There was wood but no water except melted snow. I still had enough grub to last a few days and had my thirty-two Smith and Wesson revolver and twenty cartridges that I could use to kill some rabbits. The sensible thing for me to do, I knew, was to get out of there by foot as fast as I could, but it was awful to think what all the people would say about me when it got around that I had walked home. I could tramp 75 miles south across the Pine Ridge Reservation and maybe get on the train east from there, but my feet were already blistered and frostbit. Besides it was risky for a white to be seen alone on the reservation since some of the Indians still had bad hearts. If I ever did get home, I knew I would sell out as quick as I could and go back to Iowa and get a job inside. I always wanted an easy job where I could wear good clothes and get bleached out. I was a sick bird.

The rest of that day I rested up, doctored my feet with snow, and mourned over my bad luck. The next day I packed my grub, pots, and blankets into a roll and was ready to go when I looked over my brush screen and saw a rider about 100 feet away. I recognized him as Bill Newsom, the head of a cattle-stealing crowd that operated on the White and Bad Rivers. This was the outfit that stole my Nebraska herd. He had a Winchester and a belt gun that looked like a forty-five Colt. It looked bad to me, so I kept my head down and watched. He went a little way, got off and tied his horse to a tree, took his Winchester out of the scabbard, and started looking around close like he was hunting for tracks. He moved slowlike toward my old camp. I was pretty sure he was looking for me and would take a pot shot at me if he had a chance. When he got a quarter-mile up the trail I took my roll, made a run for his horse, and got on fast. The horse was snorty and wild but I stayed with him and laid on the leather. Inside of two hours I was across White River and the scare had worn off some. I cooked the best I could and at the same time kept an eye open for any other riders. That night I found an empty dugout and stayed there. I cut through 2 feet of ice to get water, which I warmed, and washed my face for the first time in several days. There was grub there so I had biscuits, bacon, coffee, and that night I had my first good sleep in several nights.

☆   ☆   ☆

[*Sibert told of taking cattle to Chicago and said, "I suppose it was the hope of going to Chicago at shipping time that kept a good many cowboys eating dust and fighting blizzards in South Dakota."*]

It was four o'clock in the morning when I pulled into Pierre. It felt good to be in South Dakota again. The air was good, and with all their faults I liked the Dakota people. The folks in Chicago and Iowa seemed to have bad manners, and the Dakota people didn't have any at all. That is what I liked best about them. I got a ride to Foster's and was soon over to my place. The pack rats were in possession. They had filled the cook stove with dried peaches and beans and put charcoal in my hole in the floor. My horses were still around and everything was all right.

☆   ☆   ☆

The university men in the West were rated a rather queer lot. We had heard of Theodore Roosevelt, northwest of us 200 miles, as a rather locoed fellow who was called the Hoot Owl or Old Four eyes.

☆   ☆   ☆

We had an election at Lindsay on November 4. We had twenty voters and most of them got drunk that day, knocked over the table, and nearly had a good fight over who was better, Bryan or McKinley. I was a clerk, so let the stuff alone and didn't argue with anyone. We clerks stuck to crackers and sardines, and I read some of the papers that were in the post office.

☆   ☆   ☆

In the hope of finding more of our cattle, a bunch of us next went to the northwestern part of South Dakota to take part in the roundups there. This was the range where the big outfits operated. Twelve of us took about 100 saddle horses and bedrolls and went up through the reservation to Narcisse Narcelle's ranch, where we stayed two nights. We heard the wagons were working about 75 miles farther on, but no one knew where, so we went on up through an unsettled country. The first night we came to the OHO camp of the Holcombe Brothers of Rapid City, where we found two hands in charge. They fed us good, which was quite a job as we had not had any dinner. They didn't know where the big outfits were exactly but allowed they were about 75 miles on northwest.

A dim trail led northwest from there, so we followed it most of next day. None of us had ever been in that country before so had quite a sight looking at it. There were no ranchers' cabins in the whole country and it was everybody's pasture. We saw brands from the states of Montana, Wyoming, the Dakotas, and Canada. About four in the afternoon we found the outfit we were looking for. There were eight different wagons strung along a small creek, and each wagon had a day herd of 2,000 to 4,000 and from 300 to 500 saddle horses. They had been working this country all spring and had met here to get each outfit's cattle bunched to send to their home range. The whole bunch worked together for a few days going east, and we went along.

We moved on through an open country full of cattle, horses, deer, antelope, coyotes, and big gray wolves. Some of the prairie dog towns were 5 or 6 miles across.

☆   ☆   ☆

In April we dehorned the cattle and shipped everything to Chicago. The Spanish-American War helped the prices some. After paying my bills, I had a little money left and felt prosperous enough to take my first Pullman on the way back. It cost $2 and was worth it.

When I got back to Pierre that spring, I bought a thirty-dollar horse and rode out to my cabin. The pack rats had been busy, and the grub was pretty low, after visitors had come and gone all winter. Three of my horses were gone, but I found about twenty leftover cattle on Sansarc Creek. I made up my mind again to get out of the cattle business.

The sheepmen were bringing in more sheep and new ranchers were coming in every spring. Most of the new ones had their families with them, and they lived in the little log houses with sod roofs the way the rest of us lived. Those who could moved their families into Pierre for the winter so the kids could go to school. The rest of them just let the kids grow up without any schooling. It was a lonely life, and a lot of them couldn't take it. One man left for Pierre one winter day to get grub and left his wife and three children in the 14 by 14 dugout. When he got back he found the sod roof had collapsed, and the whole family was dead underneath. He dug the frozen bodies out and hauled them to Pierre for burial. It was a horrible thing to have happen—even to a sheepman.

I was pretty busy that fall taking care of the horses. For a while I herded them every day and penned them every night. As there was plenty of grass and water, they weren't hard to hold. One day when I went to the Lindsay Post Office, one of the little boys came out and said, "Bruce, you are going broke. You're crazy to buy horses. Papa said so." This was the opinion of about everybody. But I was tired of chasing cows all over South Dakota and finding half of them dead in the spring. And I sure didn't want to smell sheep all day long, year in, year out, the way some people had to do to make their living.

About this time Jeff Carr came along and made me a good offer for my place and I sold it to him. Then I bought another one about 6 miles south on Sansarc Creek. It had a small dugout on it that wasn't more than 5½ feet high. We were always bumping our heads on the roof. This can be right aggravating. One day I hired a carpenter to build me a house I could stand up in. He did a fair job and made a log house 20 by 20 with a board floor and a dirt

The XO ranch in 1900.

roof. There was even tar paper between the layers of sod, and this helped keep the rain from coming through. It was the best house I had ever had in South Dakota. After getting the corrals fixed up, we got along good.

☆   ☆   ☆

When I went west in 1890 as a floating laborer, South Dakota was pretty raw and so was I. I first went under the name of Mort, changed it to Wallace DeLong and was called "Walrus," and then back to my real name when I went to Pierre. This was the custom, as so many who went out there were just one jump ahead of the sheriff. Up to that time I had done nothing worse than raiding a watermelon patch, but thought it proper to change my name anyway.

Siberts's horse herd in 1900.

118

After ten years in South Dakota I had gone up in the world some. I owned a wagon, mower, rake, a 20 by 20 log house with a floor, and had 150 horses. At the Pierre bank I owed $1,000. Horses had about doubled in price the last year or two, and my herd nearly doubled every year. Of course, most of my profits were just paper profits as a horse doesn't have much of a sale until it is three or four years old. But anyway, I was doing pretty good.

☆　　　☆　　　☆

[*Sibert was forced to "hole up," he put it, in a dugout during a winter storm.*]

A dugout is about the worst-looking kind of a house that can be found anywhere, but it is fine in a pinch. Rudy's place looked desolate there in the middle of the prairies, but I was in a pinch so tied my team and went in to see about bedding down there. When I lit the candle and got a fire going, it looked better. The grub box had baking powder, salt pork, coffee, and beans in it, enough for a real meal. I got out the ax and chopped through a foot of ice to water the team before I put them in the hay corral for the night. After getting the place warm and eating my supper of sow belly and biscuits, I pulled off my cold leather boots and got comfortable. After I rolled a cigaret, I looked over Rudy's books. He was a Princeton man and had Marcus Aurelius, Dickens, and Boccaccio to read when he was there alone. I picked Boccaccio and pretty nearly forgot to go to bed that night.

To pass the time away I spent part of it in Pierre that winter. To make loafing easier, I dabbled in the wheat market at a bucket shop and after making $500, lost it and more too. I took a trip to Minneapolis and saw a good horseshow for trotters, pacers, and ponies. Dan Patch, the fastest harness horse at that time, and some Hackneys, a nobby, stylish breed, also performed. Minneapolis had some good stage shows. I saw *Ben Hur,* which had real horses running on a treadmill, and others. After losing my money in the grain pit, I decided to go back to the sagebrush country where I belonged.

In that big country west of the Missouri we never saw anything but the cabins of ranchers before 1902. Then the claim shacks began to show up on the level land near the trails and roads. The wool-hat people with their kids and plows had come. Some of the ranchers tried to hold on to the water holes and the

Bruce and Rose Siberts at the XO ranch house.

hay bottoms by hiring somebody to file on them. The going price was $200 for building an 8 by 10 shack and putting a stove and a cot in it. Then there were others who made a claim in order to sell out to anybody who came along. Some boasted they had never slept on their claim at all, and the Land Office never pried much into such personal affairs. After Teddy Roosevelt became president, I heard there were quite a lot of prosecutions for fraud, but I never saw many convicted around me for making a final proof out of just plain blue sky. But the sodbusters, including a lot of schoolteachers out to pick up some change, were there to stay, and the wide-open prairie that we had used for free pasture was on the way out forever.

The free range was getting pinched, not only by the homesteaders but also because there were too many mouths to feed on the prairie that was left. The cattlemen hadn't made any money for years, so they quit one by one. Some went back east, some went into business in town, and others moved their herds up to Canada and started out again there. Very few had a fortune when they folded up. The sheepmen had always done better than the cattlemen, but they felt the same squeeze west of the Missouri after about 1904 or 1905.

I had been doing all right with horses. The cold crop was good every year, and the prices had done pretty well after the Boer War sent them up. In June, 1902, I shipped a carload to DeWitt, Iowa, and averaged between $50 and $75 apiece. They were sold at an auction back of a saloon, and I'll admit that the drinks helped some. That August I tried it again but didn't do so well. There had been a ballgame at DeWitt the day before, and it had ended up in a fight. This hurt my sale, so I decided to try some other place after that.

In the fall of 1904 I shipped two carloads to East St. Louis, the biggest horse market in the world at that time. They had pens for thousands of horses and sold several carloads a week to buyers from all over the world as well as from the East. While I was there, I went to see the World's Fair in St. Louis. It was not quite as big as the one in Chicago in 1893, but there was still lots to see and a lot of walking to do. I had my first ride in an automobile bus that toured the fairgrounds, and even though it cost $2, I thought it had something on a horse for sight-seeing. Back in Pierre with $2,000 for the forty-five broncs, I could now look even the banker in the eye.

Back at my XO Ranch on the Sansarc it seemed lonesome without the horses, even if I had some pretty girls as neighbors. I had a buggy and hauled the homesteaders around some. Rose Woodard and I seemed to hit it off the best. One night after staying at her claim until quite late, I went to sleep driving home. When I woke up the team was running in circles at a fast clip. I was afraid of a spill, but they finally ran down and stopped.

On the night of December 13, 1905, Rose and I were married in the Methodist parsonage at Pierre. The next morning when we got on the train to go to Omaha, Scotty Phillips, who had the buffaloes, was on. He called Rose "Mrs. Siberts," which seemed to shock her. We doubled back to Colorado to look around for a ranch to buy, but finding it cold and snowy there, we decided to go on south. I had heard that oil had been discovered in Oklahoma so went to Okmulgee and bought a place 25 miles south of the first big oil pool. I figured one might raise some oil as well as horses in a place like that. Besides, it had the best water I had tasted in the south, and I was tired of alkali after living fifteen years in South Dakota.

It is all over now. As I look over the 8,000 acres in Oklahoma land I have now and think about the days when I lived in my little cabin on the Sansarc, I can see that it was horses that gave me my start. If I had stayed in cattle, I might still have been drinking alkali water and living with a mortgage in South Dakota. But it wasn't a bad place for a young man to start out—even if there was nothing but prairie and sky.

COUNTRY EDITOR

Ira Nichols

HE WAS SUED *eight times for libel. If there was a fight he was in the thick of it. If there wasn't a fight he would likely provoke one. His was a tireless effort to get the upper hand over his opposition. He relished trading near-slanderous barbs with his neighboring editors.*

Ira Nichols was not typical of the country editor at the turn of the century. But he epitomized the extremes which characterized many editors of that era.

Printer-editors followed close on the heels of the earliest settlers. They were out to make a buck, but frequently they were persons of pronounced convictions whose delight was adding spice to community life, sometimes at the risk of life or limb. For a look at their life-style we turn to Nichols and one of his several privately printed books, Forty Years of Rural Journalism in Iowa. *His career centered around Iowa Falls, Iowa, from 1895 to 1933.*

Nichols enrolled at Iowa State College in 1886 and his recollections of those days recall a slice of early Americana.

The work ethic was his god. He spoke approvingly of the merchant who went to his store at seven o'clock in the morning and worked well into the night, six days a week. He followed the same pattern, accumulated modest wealth and educated his family, none of whom chose to follow his pattern. So he sold his paper in the depression of 1933 and lived to criticize everything that the paper did for another quarter of a century.

Nevertheless, when the Iowa Falls papers marked the town's centennial, they identified Ira as the most significant person to have been in that Hardin County community during its first one hundred years.

The excerpts from the book mentioned are largely concerned with newspapering. But the first piece has to do with the old-time livery barn, just because it paints so vivid a picture of an establishment that was of great importance in early day communities. Nichols's father owned the livery barn in Glidden, Iowa. The son watched over the establishment at night.

THE PIONEER LIVERY BARN

HERE it stood, the pioneer livery barn. The palatial office was some 8 or 10 feet square. At one side was a small bed, filled with straw some years before. The ventilation was superb, like unto the odors of the barn and the vermin and the bugs and the dust and the must and the tobacco fumes and the expectorations. There was one little window to let in the sunshine and the light. The little old heating stove was set up in the center of a great spittoon, a box 3 feet square, filled with ashes. Here sat in the winter evenings the ancient board of strategy, pipes, chewing tobacco, and euchre deck, mulling over the latest community scandal, solving the affairs of state, passing upon the beauties and defects of women, critically commenting upon the latest pugilistic prowess of John L. Sullivan. Hanging on the walls were great buffalo coats and blankets used on long rides in the bitter cold.

Just back of the office was the oat bin and just beyond the oat bin was the corncrib, feeding place for rats. Back of the crib was the well and on beyond the well, a number of horse stalls. Opposite the office, bin, crib, well, and stalls, on the other side of a gangway, was a long row of horse stalls. In this part of the barn were kept the livery or driving horses. There were two wings to the barn, also filled with horse stalls, except part of the right wing which was used for buggies and sleighs. Over the center of the barn was a large haymow, from whence the hay was put down in the racks above the horses' heads.

Along beside the livery and feed barn was another large feed barn, almost an exact counterpart of the main barn, except that it had no crib, well, or office. It held forty-eight horses. In the two barns could be housed seventy-two horses. The price of a meal for

123

a team was 25 cents. If a team were kept overnight and fed, the price was 75 cents, that is, 25 cents for supper, 25 cents for lodging, and 25 cents for breakfast. The charge for furnishing a stall and hay for a team at the noon hour was 10 cents.

☆   ☆   ☆

It is past the midnight hour and the great army of rats have come forth from their lairs. The boy in the office, keeping nightly vigil, arises from his pallet of boards, pitchfork in hand, goes quietly out, scoots the pitchfork along the floor amid a score of rats, scampering to every cover. Now and then a rat is impaled, squealing on the fork tines.

It is along toward midnight and a strange noise awakens the boy from his nightly slumbers. He goes forth, lantern dimly burning, perhaps some horse, in from a long and hard drive, has the colic, perhaps there is need of a whiskey sling or sweet milk and molasses or niter, also the drenching bottle. It is the lad's duty to sally forth and keep vigil over his flock. He looks about from place to place. The horses are all well, lying down or champing their hay. Still, there is that strange noise. It comes now from a far stall, some wild animal perhaps. The boy arms himself with the pitchfork and peers carefully about. A drunken fool has taken possession of the stall, taken up his bed, moaning in elysian dreams and fitful pains. Let him sleep it off. He is harmless. The boy returns to his bed of boards, sleeps as soon as he touches the boards. There is a pounding and hallooing at the office window. Three denizens of the prairie, patronizers of some blind pig, jug in hand, wobbly kneed, maudlin mouthed, want their bronchoes. The boy gets up and gets their team, hitches it up for them, little concerned; drunken fools are his daily diet.

☆   ☆   ☆

The keeper of the pioneer livery had no fear of man or brute or devil. Drunks, tramps, bums, pretty thieves, gamblers, swindlers, horse jockeys, and traders were his common stock and store.

Stabling and feeding horses was an important part of the livery barn business. Teams brought grain to market from far distances, stopped for hay and water and feed, stopped for the night. Teams came from inland villages carrying freight and

IRA NICHOLS

Ira Nichols epitomized the old-time country editor who thrived on controversy.

human kind. Teams came in with mail from star routes across the prairies. All times of day and night teams and men came and went.

Along toward night the prairie schooner hove in sight. Cooped up in the wagon were the family, with all their worldly possessions, wanting a little feed or water, few clothes and little or no money, destination far away. The children in rags peered out from under the flaps of the cover to the wagon, mothers in torn and worn calico dresses kept well out of sight, fathers, long-bearded, uncouth, hardened, asked for a bundle of hay or a peck of oats. Ah, what tales of sorrow, broken hopes, and privations those lonely schooner wagons could tell. The families had gone west in the 1870s and early 1880s in covered wagons with all their earthly possessions, leading or driving their horses and cattle, hauling a few farm utensils, camping on the prairies. They were seeking new land and new homes in Kansas, Nebraska, and Dakota. They built sodhouses and broke up the wild lands and put in their simple crops. They were up against new conditions and their methods of farming in the east would not do in their new homes.

They made the fight for a few years with little to eat, little to wear, and few or no school facilities. Every spring there came new hope and every summer they prayed and prayed for rain that never came or came too late. They watched in tears and sorrow the grain that withered and died.

In the late 1880s, every fall great numbers of these poor, miserable, God-forsaken families trekked back through Iowa, eastward bound, to find food and shelter among relatives or with old-time neighbors.

In the long nights of winter came the public dance with all its frills and fancies, came the teams from far and near, filled the long rows of stalls, came in bobsleds, came in cutters, filled the town with drunks and joy-seekers. The livery boy kept his nightly vigil, watching the horses, watching the boozers. Along toward the hours of morning, after the dancing and lovemaking and boozing had had full swing, the Beau Brummels returned for their teams; stopped in the little cooped up office; spat upon the floor; took another swig of liquor; rehearsed their smutty, dirty stories; tried to steal a better whip; and then departed.

From Carroll, throughout the years, came the 10:10 train at night. There was no such thing as bed or closing the barn before this train came in. In the early days of Iowa prohibition, Glidden

All strata of society had a common meeting place in the old livery stable—horse traders, sharpies, drunks looking for a warm place to sleep, business and professional people who, like everyone else, depended upon the horse for transportation over the prairies and the mud roads.

was dry and Carroll was wet. Every day men left their teams in the livery barn and went to Carroll after liquor, perhaps doing some other business, returning on the 10:10 train, sometimes sober, often drunk, sometimes silly, often mean and quarrelsome. The livery barn was headquarters for all such gentry and each week one of the chores was to take a bushel basket and gather up the empty liquor bottles.

Such are some of the stories of the old-time livery barn, now gone, well nigh forgotten.

☆   ☆   ☆

COLLEGE DAYS IN THE 1880s

Higher education in the 1880s in Iowa was quite primitive. I was the first person from my community in western Iowa to graduate from the agricultural college at Ames, Iowa.

The Ames college catalogue, a rather simple pamphlet, was obtained and pored over. There was the item of board and room at $2.10 per week in the cottages and $2.25 per week in the main building. The saving of the fifteen cents per week was a matter of debate. Finally, it was decided that $2.10 was enough. There was the janitor's fee of $4 or $5 per semester, a small charge for breakage, and $5 to $10 per semester for textbooks. The total charge for these items per semester was around $50. Then there was the carfare back and forth from home at the beginning and end of the semester, laundry, and incidentals.

The whole amount of expense for a semester was figured at around $60 to $65. The total maximum cost for a whole year was placed at $125. At this rate a four-year course could be had at $500.

The college year started during the latter part of February and ended in November, with a month's summer vacation, the purpose being to give the students an opportunity to teach school in the winter and to earn money with which to pay their college expenses.

Around February 22, 1886, there was much excitement in our humble home. It was time for me to leave for college. There was no money to buy a trunk and so mother's old trunk was gotten out and filled with books, bedding, and such clothing as we had. The lid to the trunk was loose and detached, but we tied the trunk up with a rope and made it safe for the journey. It was thought best to be on hand early in the morning of the first day of school and so the night train was taken. The train left at 10:10 and arrived at Ames around one o'clock in the night. We waited around the waiting room at the depot and in the little barroom of the little hotel until morning. It was something over a mile to the college and the only way out was by horse bus or foot. I made arrangements to have my trunk taken out and then walked out to save the bus fare.

Ah, that first room! It was located in the "old cottage," upstairs, midway of the building, and facing the north. The furniture consisted of a cot, a chair, a simple table, a little sheet iron heating stove, and a kerosene lamp. Down beside the building was a huge pile of cordwood. I went down and sawed enough wood for the night and built a fire in the little stove, a miserably little thing. I unpacked my trunk and got out the bedding and made a bed on the cot. Snow had been falling most of the day and the darkness of night came down upon me. I lit the little lamp and stood at the window and gazed out on the night and on the snow that scurried about in drifts and an utter feeling of loneliness came

This was Old Main at the Iowa Agricultural College when Ira Nichols came to college in 1886. The north wing of this building burned in 1900 and the remaining wing burned in 1902. The cornerstone of New Main (Central Building) was laid in 1905 but it was not named Beardshear until thirty-five years later.

over me. I knew no one, I had never been away from home, and a terrible feeling of homesickness took possession of my soul and I thought I was going to die. If I ever lived until morning, I was going home as fast as I could get there. The night dragged on but morning came, as mornings always follow the night, and the sun shone resplendent on the newly fallen snow, and the loneliness vanished with the work of the day.

IOWA STATE HISTORY COLLECTION

☆　　　　☆　　　　☆

Life at the Iowa Agricultural College in 1886 was interesting to the novice. No one was allowed to leave the campus without the special permission of the president. Chapel was held each day at 5:15 P.M. and on each Sunday morning. Everyone was required to attend. Each student was assigned a seat and the proctors went along, registry books in hand, and checked each saint and sinner. Each vacant seat was recorded and the absentee must report to the president and get excused and about the only excuse was illness.

When Ira Nichols came to Iowa Agricultural College in 1886 he stayed in the "old cottage" shown in lower left just over the smokestacks of Old Main from which this picture was taken. He chose the cottage rather than Old Main because it was 15 cents per week cheaper—$2.10 versus $2.25! That was for board and room! This picture looks southwest from the present location of Beardshear and the second building from the upper right (with mansard roof) still stands! It is known as the Mechanics Laboratory.

132

Each evening in the early spring and late fall at seven o'clock and in the summer at seven-thirty o'clock, the proctors checked each room to see that the inmates were in their accustomed places ready for study. At ten o'clock each evening all lights went out and everyone must be in bed.

Strict attendance at classes was required. With the exception of four weeks spent in the college hospital with a broken bone, I never missed a class or a chapel service in four years. If a student were absent from class and called upon to recite, a zero was recorded. A few zeros was apt to mean failure to pass.

☆   ☆   ☆

With the exception of a few students living in Ames, all students roomed and boarded at the college, either in the "Old Main" building, or the "old cottage," or the "new cottage." Each student had a certain seat at a certain table and ate there for a semester at least. For four years we knew fairly well just what the bill of fare would be for each meal and each season. On Monday morning there was always hash and boiled eggs. There was pie twice each week, beans on a certain day, and so on. Grapes were served from the college vineyard in the fall and strawberries from the horticultural gardens in June. There was plenty of milk and cream. The college farm kept 100 cows, which were milked by students, 10 cows per student, 4 cents per day per cow for pay. This meant 40 cents per day for the student, which would pay his school expenses. There were around 400 students, 75 girls and 325 boys, and 100 cows were sufficient.

There was military drill on Wednesdays and Fridays and the Friday session ended up with a dress parade, in which the companies assembled in line on the campus facing the Old Main building. Captain J. R. Lincoln, well known in later years and a general in the regular army, was commandant. He had served in the Confederate army and was a good drill master. There was rivalry among the student captains of the different companies and much company drilling during recreation hours and Saturdays. One of the captains was E. A. Kreger who was judge advocate of the United States Army during the World War. The girls had a company which the commandant drilled and was considered the best drilled company on the campus. This, however, did not deter the boys from dubbing them the broom brigade.

☆   ☆   ☆

The faculty at Ames in the 1880s was looked upon with considerable awe and much respect. Leigh Hunt was the president in the spring of 1886. He was a polished young man of much ability. [Hunt was president from 1885 to 1886.] He later became in a way a world citizen. He went first to Seattle, where he edited a daily paper and gained wide attention. Later he developed large mines in China and cotton fields in Egypt and at times was the possessor of large fortunes.

Professor [Edgar W.] Stanton was perhaps the most beloved instructor. I took college algebra, geometry, trigonometry, analytical geometry, calculus, commercial law, and five semesters of economics under him. A. S. Welch, the first president of the institution, was still a part of the school. He taught psychology and the English sentence. He had written a book on the English sentence which was used as a textbook [*The Sentence, a Psychology for Teachers*].

Looking back over the vista of the years, those college days bring many pleasant memories. Ah, the woods and the fields, the flowers and the butterflies, the herbarium work in botany, the bug collection in entomology, the laboratory work, the unfolding of new volumes of thought, the earning of a little spending money by sawing wood or working on the farm at 10 cents per hour, the burning longing for the home visit at the end of the semester, the routine of study and recitation, the smile of an instructor for work well done, the recreation hour games, the college pranks, the friendship of students, the dining halls where the students gathered three times daily, the lectures by noted men, the college literary societies, yea, even the daily chapel. Ah, the associations, the training, the discipline, and the garnered help for afteryears!

THE GLIDDEN *GRAPHIC*

Along around 1890, Glidden, Iowa, had two newspapers, the Glidden *Success* and the Glidden *Graphic*. The *Success* was a six-column quarto with two pages of home print. The paper was printed on an Army press, which turned with a crank and worked about like the wringer of a washing machine. The type form was cranked on a track, back and forth, under a rubber roller that was pressed down upon the type with a spring. The type was inked by a boy with a hand roller. The *Graphic* was a seven-column folio paper, all home print, and of course changed the Glidden *Success* into a Glidden failure. The *Graphic* was edited by "Paddy Ford," an old soldier and an experienced printer. He came down to the office each morning, rolled up his sleeves, and started to work at a brisk gait. After working a short time, he lit his pipe and worked awhile longer, when he remarked that a man could not work and smoke at the same time and so he sat down and smoked. Two papers in a little town of a few hundred people was nothing uncommon fifty years ago. Grundy Center, Iowa, a town of some 1,200 persons in 1890, at one time had four papers.

My first move in the *Graphic* office was to dispense with a $10 per week foreman and to take the job myself. I figured that I could write six or seven columns of local news and two or three columns of editorial each week, gather the news, take care of the advertising, keep the books, make the collections, pay the bills, set the advertising and job work, and do the press work alone, and I did. My sister came into the office and learned to set type and with some help from me was soon able to get up ten or twelve columns of reading matter each week.

Two full columns of solid eight point was a fair day's work by hand composition at the case. There was now and then a compositor that could set three columns per day part of the time. Putting it another way, a 13-em line of type per minute was about all that any hand compositor could set. Distributing the type back in the case took about an hour to a column. Linotype composition is about six times as fast as hand composition, but linotype composition was unknown in the country press in the 1890s.

☆   ☆   ☆

In those days there was little composition on advertising. Most advertising ran without change the year around and answered the purpose of signboards. Modern propaganda was undiscovered. The patent medicine companies were on the job with their nostrums, exploiting human ignorance and suffering. They paid from $10 to $20 per year for their advertising in the weekly press. Their advertisements consisted mostly of testimonials by readers. Some of the newspaper boys bunched the patent medicine readers and ran short reading notices between them in order to comply with the contract. Over the whole bunch they ran some such head as "Hints on Health."

☆   ☆   ☆

All the little towns had two banks and each town had two fac-
tions that rallied around their favorite banks. In every town election one bank would be on one side and the other bank on the
other side. The little newspaper always had a difficult problem to
keep from being ground to pieces on the nether stone. This was
especially true if the newspaper owed one of the banks. Many a
newspaperman in an early day lost out because he opposed the
bank that he owed. I resolved in the very beginning that I would
not become obligated to a bank by borrowing money of it, a
resolution that I religiously kept to the end of my newspaper days.

IOWA FALLS—MAY, 1895, TO JANUARY, 1900

When I sold my interest in the Glidden *Graphic,* I chose Iowa
Falls, which, in the end, proved to be the best field for a
newspaper. I took possession of the Hardin County *Citizen* May
2, 1895, and issued my first newspaper on May 11, 1895. It was
not much of a paper. I certainly was a hopeless specimen, with a
smattering of everything and a proficiency in nothing. I was
neither an editor nor a printer nor a salesman nor a newsman nor
a businessman.

The country was in the midst of one of its major depressions,
but I did not know it.

I had contracted to pay $500 every six months for five suc-
cessive payments on the purchase price of the plant, and the debt
was secured by a chattel mortgage. My total income during the
summer months of 1895 was only around $125 per month, out of
which must be paid help, rent, ready-prints, living, and so forth.

The advertising rate was 10 cents per inch. All type had to be
set by hand. I, personally, had to set the advertising and job work,
to gather the local news and to write it, to prepare the editorial, to
make up the forms, to feed presses, to help with hand composition on the newspaper, to build fires, to sweep floors, to clean and
overhaul machinery, to keep books, to make out the bills, to make
collections, and to judiciously distribute the proceeds in such
manner as would best appease the creditors. In fact, there was
nothing that was not apt to fall to my lot. Within a year or so I
found time to canvass in the country for new subscribers one or
two days per week. Sometimes I went on foot, sometimes on a
bicycle, sometimes with a horse. Of course, this volume of work

falling on me required constant toil from seven o'clock in the morning to ten and eleven o'clock at night.

I ran a newspaper for fifteen years before I thought well of buying a typewriter. I always whipped the salesman with the statement that I could write longhand faster than I could think, which was true.

The Hardin County *Citizen* had fifteen direct competitors, namely, the Alden *Times,* the Williams *Wasp,* the Radcliffe *Signal,* the Hubbard *Monitor,* the Eldora *Herald,* the Eldora *Ledger,* the Eldora *Enterprise,* the Ackley *Phonograph,* the Ackley *World,* the Dows *Advocate,* the Iowa Falls *Sentinel,* the Hampton *Recorder,* the Hampton *Globe,* and the Hampton *Chronicle.* A year's subscription to these papers ranged from 25 cents to $1, and prices changed from time to time and from place to place. For instance, in the Cottage neighborhood, a highly competitive place among newspapers, the current rate for Eldora and Iowa Falls and Hubbard papers was 50 cents per year.

My first competitor in Iowa Falls was Charles Elliott. He had conducted some sort of a newspaper contest in conjunction with Ellsworth College and had added some eighty to ninety subscribers to his list in Ellis Township, which took most of the township. Soon after I came to Iowa Falls Elliott sold his paper to Platt. In the fall of 1897 I sent Frank Stoddard out into Ellis to break up this block of *Sentinel* readers. Stoddard was an old soldier, a very keen and intelligent man, and a well-known citizen.

Well, Stoddard shifted seventy of the *Sentinel* subscribers, the shift taking place January 1, when their subscriptions to the *Sentinel* expired. The shifts dragged along through January and the longer they dragged the uglier Platt became. Finally, along in February he invited Stoddard up to his office and Stoddard made the mistake of accepting the invitation. I heard some loud talking across the hall, also pulling and hauling and grunting. By the time I got to the door Platt was pushing and kicking Stoddard down the stairway. When he turned to come back, he was furious, and I crept back into my den.

Stoddard had Platt arrested on a charge of assault and battery and the case was tried to a jury. Platt and Stoddard acted as their own attorneys. Platt won and immediately led the jury to the nearest drugstore to set up the treats for the peers who had kept his armor unsullied. However, the whole affair did Platt and his paper no good, for the public sympathized with Stoddard.

Strictly a period picture. In Ira Nichols's writings he painted a glowing picture of the accomplishments of the early-day businessmen in the Iowa Falls community and spoke disdainfully of the "chain store and filling station era." Four of these six men were on hand when Iowa Falls came into being in 1855. All six were figures of consequence when Nichols began his newspapering days in Iowa Falls in 1895. From left to right (seated), J. T. Lane, T. J. McChesney, J. S. Smith, O. E. Abel and (standing), William Burgess and L. O. Bliss.

☆ ☆ ☆

In 1895 the Populist party was strong in the Dakotas, Nebraska, and Kansas, and there were a few Populists in Iowa. Like most new parties, the Populists were much ridiculed by the old parties, and I, as a Republican, joined in the performance to some extent. One day in came a man, a Populist at the time, 6 feet

2 inches tall, looking over his specs at me and pointing his big fist and finger in my face, who said: "Young man, I want you to keep your leaky old proboscis out of my political soup kettle." It was K. C. (Kitt) (Napoleon) Curtis of Ellis Township. Everybody knew Kitt but I didn't. Curtis was a unique character. He buttressed his many sayings with scriptural quotations and had a knack of settling an argument with a single sentence, to which there was no reply. In later years Kitt was the chief of police in Iowa Falls. One day he was standing on a street corner, looking off into space, when a dog came up and bit his leg. Kitt peered down at the dog, reached down with both hands, picked the canine up, raised it far above his head, slammed it down on the cement walk, and there was no dog. About this time, a lady, the owner of the dog, began to berate Kitt for killing the animal. The reply was: "Great God, madam, do you think my leg was meant for dog meat?" What could the woman say in rebuttal?

☆ ☆ ☆

In the winter of 1899 I determined to increase the subscription price of my newspaper from $1.00 to $1.50, thinking that I had made enough improvement in the paper to stand the strain. I set April 1 for the date of advance, thinking that the farmers would be going into the fields and would pay little attention to my little performance, which proved to be true for the time being. However, on the first day of the next January, when time for renewals came, trouble began. For forty days I lost daily three time-tried and fire-tested subscribers. This was destroying my 1,100 list pretty rapidly. I did not like to see them going over to the other newspaper. Something had to be done. I stopped the whole performance dead in its tracks with just one front page article, less than a column long. Great is the power of an idea. I counted all the news items in each paper in the country and found that the *Citizen,* in the week under discussion, had 724 items, while all the other papers in the county combined had only 543. The *Citizen* cost $1.50 and the combined subscription rate of all the other papers in the county with which I competed was $9.00. In other words, speaking figuratively, it cost $9.00 to get 543 pounds of flour of my nine competitors, while one could buy 724 pounds of flour of the *Citizen* for $1.50. The argument was 100 percent effective.

☆ ☆ ☆

In my first years in Iowa Falls the town marshal raided a poker game and arrested the players and the proprietor of the place. In those days card playing was considered quite an offense, gave the preachers something to preach about, and gave the colonial dames a field for action. Raiding poker dens was a common pastime. Of course, the offense was mostly in the tribal head. There is no more harm in playing with a deck of cards than there is in playing with a croquet set, unless you make harm of it. However, neither gambling with cards nor on horseraces adds much to the welfare of society. I wrote the police raid up and brought onto the printed page the names of the persons arrested. After the paper came out, the taker of the "drop" at the poker table stopped me on the street and gave me to understand that unless I attended to my own business my life was just not exactly safe. The threat did not scare me much, but it started me to thinking. Sometime later I wrote up a divorce action, giving publication to too many allegations and to too much debatable detail. This got me into trouble and jolted up my thinking apparatus some more.

A heinous crime was committed at Charles City and a mob took the culprit or culprits from jail and hung him or them to a bridge until dead. Looking at the terrible murder committed by the victims of the mob, I wrote an editorial note justifying the mob. The paper came out Friday morning and long about noon I heard somebody with a cane coming up the steps, thump, thump, thump. It was Judge Silas M. Weaver coming to give me a much needed lesson in good citizenship. He explained to me: that the mob is the tribe acting in the role of anarchists, maniacs, and murderers; that the mob is the frightful destroyer of orderly government; that the life and property of no person, guilty or innocent, is safe with a mob at large; and that any newspaper condoning mob violence is aiding and abetting the destruction of government, aiding and abetting lawlessness, aiding and abetting destruction of property, aiding and abetting murder. This and more he told me. I listened silently with much humiliation of spirit and learned a lesson that lasted through life.

☆   ☆   ☆

THE CAMPAIGN

During the political campaigns there was much talking on both sides. Each side marched to the attack. Ten thousand libels and slanders were uttered, but no one ever thought much about

140

suing for libel or slander. Men were expected to stand punishment as well as to administer it. This was no place and time for cry-babies. The Ackley *Phonograph,* for example, contained a column article devoted to the editor of the Hardin County *Citizen* in which the *Citizen* editor was charged with having been "born in a bawdy-house, with being an offspring of a canine of uncertain parentage, with feeding on patent nostrums, and with being a victim of self-abuse," all of which served as a good joke, added to the gaity of nations, and hurt no one, except perhaps the author of the article. To give an idea of the campaign, a few of the political items and articles are here reproduced, with the names of persons sometimes left out.

The "anti-ring" Republicans are a fist full of filibusters, firing, furious, foaming, frenzied Philistines and political bushwhackers, who, the Iowa Falls papers say, "are bent on demolishing, disrupting, and destroying."—Ackley *Phonograph.*

This paper would like to see a few fellows, working in conjunction with and surrepticiously [*sic*] defending the tax-ferret gang, come out like men and openly fight.—*Citizen.*

Fifty dollars each to certain ward-heelers, 145 dinners, 3,000 cigars, and 24 large kegs of beer in one precinct is a pretty good showing for ring methods, is it not?—Eldora *X-Ray.*

The Hubbard *Monitor* wants to know if a mixture of Republicans and Democrats can cleanse politics. We want to know if a mixture of boodlers, secret contractors, and confidence men can do it? Is there any reason to suppose that they will do it?—*Citizen.*

It was sort of mean for the ever irrepressible John Roberts of Ackley to say that he would rather be in h—l without an introduction than in Eldora for an hour.—*Citizen.*

Our friend of the *Herald* thinks that the agony will soon be over. "Agony!" What's the matter with you? This is just a summer picnic carried over into the autumn days. Look pleasant and be happy.—*Citizen.*

Just think of the bellowing menagerie that is now making a specialty of constituting the Republican party of Hardin

In the Ira Nichols era, printers spent much of their time hunched over a drawer of type, picking out one character at a time and then similarly redistributing the type once the paper or print job was complete. Tom J. White, a printer for sixty-six years, shown at his typecase in Jefferson, Iowa.

142

County; Mr. A., a mongrel Democratic deserter; Mr. B., another half-breed with a white-line record; Mr. C., a poor old man who has sinned away his life grinding axes for men who despise him; Mr. D., who has been promised the office of recorder in exchange for his newspaper support; Mr. E., who still has $7,000 of Hardin County's money; Mr. F., who is one of the authors of the "secret contract"; Mr. H., who refuses to tell the people about that $22,000 that has dwindled away to $2,958.32; Mr. I., who refuses to tell the people the truth regarding that primary expense account. And then there are others. And these are the men who howl and brand as bolters honest men who refuse to assist in covering up their rotten deeds.—*Citizen*. [The actual names were used in this article.]

On the one side is tax-ferretism, rotten primaries, and party prostitutors. On the other side is decency, good citizenship, and men who do not believe that public office is a private graft. There are two flags: The black flag of party prostitution, tax-ferretism, and rotten primaries; and the stars and stripes of good citizenship. The voters must decide under which flag they will enlist.—*Citizen*.

The mighty wail about the bolters and the villification [*sic*] of Mitterer must not deceive the voter for a minute. This howl is made to conceal the issues at stake. The grafters do not care to meet the record.—*Citizen*.

All the beating of tom-toms and howling made by the gang of grafters center around two points and only two. One is that you are a dirty, nasty set of bolters, and the other is the villification [*sic*] of Mitterer. They make no answer to the charges of rotten primaries, tax-ferretism, party prostitution, and stock-foodism. There will be no answer. But they hope to divert the attention of the public from the real issues at stake by uttering a continuous wail against Mitterer and the bolters. For the purpose of keeping the real issues before the voters, we repeat the article of last week on "Points to Consider." We do not want the people to forget the real issues for a moment. The success of this band of grafters depends on their ability to conceal their identity.—*Citizen*.

The frenzy and froth of the *Citizen* quill-pusher is agonizing. He will have to be committed to the asylum for the feeble-minded before the campaign is over. He can't distinguish between personal abuse and legitimate argument. He never relished brain food, but his diet is evidently stale buttermilk, spoiled pickles, etc. Say, Nick, wash the dirt out of your ears just once, scrub your filthy teeth, and change the socks that you have worn all summer, and you will look and smell better. Then you can turn you attention to filling the empty cavity in your cranium. The *Phonograph* deprecates personalities; however, if the upstart does not desist from his sewer effusions, we will turn aside from our usual course to kick the mangy cur. Mitterer's official record is as noisome as the *Citizen's* method of defending it. Funk's editorship of the *Citizen* invites retaliatory measures.—Ackley *Phonograph*.

☆   ☆   ☆

Eugene S. Ellsworth was born in Milwaukee in 1848 and came with his father to Iowa Falls in 1866. The son drove the livery teams over the prairies in this part of Iowa and became interested in the possibilities of Iowa farmlands. In 1870 Eugene Ellsworth opened up a land and loan office in Iowa Falls, which he continued during the remainder of his life. When the B. C. R. & N. railway was built, he was one of the directors and one of the stockholders in the Town Lot Company that laid out the town sites between Iowa Falls and Estherville. In a general way Ellsworth amassed his large fortune through the advance in the price of real estate and in making real estate loans.

During the years of Ellsworth's active life the value of farmlands in Iowa, Minnesota, and the Dakotas rapidly advanced in price. He was forever buying land at one price and selling it at a higher price, and he had large land holdings in many states. It was said at one time that his farmlands, placed quarter section against quarter section, would reach from Iowa Falls to the Canadian line. This may or may not have been overdrawn but it gave some indication of the volume of his real estate business.

When I came to Iowa Falls, the firm of Ellsworth & Jones had offices in Iowa Falls, Chicago, Boston, and Crookston, Minnesota. A large force of office and field men were employed.

The firm gave my printing office enough job printing to keep one man busy and added much to my financial comfort. George Pyle was the proofreader for Ellsworth & Jones. In those days all type was handset and letters would become battered. If any letter had a scratch on it, Mr. Pyle would be sure to find it. He was blind in one eye, but he could see entirely too much with the other eye. The office force nicknamed him "Eagle Eye." To give some idea of the volume of the firm's loan business, my office printed 2,000 farm loan applications every sixty days. Ellsworth & Jones

This was a scene in the back shop of Ira Nichols's newspaper in Iowa Falls when advertisements and headlines were all handset. Shown left to right, Minnie Thomas, Julia Taylor, and Jake Sanders.

had farm loans covering most of northern Iowa, southern Minnesota, and the Red River valley. These loans were usually taken at 6 or 7 percent and sold for ½ or 1 percent less. This gave Ellsworth & Jones a constant interest income on these loans of ½ to 1 percent. The firm used to advertise that they never had had to foreclose a mortgage.

Ellsworth was a man of determination, persistence, restless energy, and vision. He contributed thousands of dollars almost without end to the buildings and equipment of Ellsworth College, took up the college deficits, and endowed the institution with 4,992 acres of Iowa land. He built the Metropolitan opera house, furnished much of the money for the public library and Ellsworth hospital, erected a number of fine business blocks, built the Ellsworth stone crusher and dam for power purposes, and at the time of his death was getting ready to erect a large hotel.

☆   ☆   ☆

There was a human side to Ellsworth that always appealed to me as a young fellow feeling my way. When he was raising

$70,000 for Ellsworth College, he walked into my humble office and gently told me what my allotment was. It was fair, I asked no question, and I signed the paper. When he personally wanted a job of printing, he gave it to me, said nothing about price, and went on his way.

On one Saturday night in February, 1907, I was working in my office about nine o'clock in the evening when Ellsworth came in. He was extremely angry. One of his old friends and coworkers had testified against him in a land condemnation suit in court. This did not set well and Ellsworth had written an article for the newspaper paying his respects to the gentleman in question in no unmistakable language. I did not blame him much and the article was pretty well written. However, I knew that it was not best to publish it and I knew that it was not well to argue the point. So I accepted the article and put it in the office safe, where it remained for many years. Ellsworth died before the next paper came out. In afteryears one day I looked the article over, still wondering whether to keep it as a keepsake. Finally I decided that it better be destroyed, so I burned it. With the death of Ellsworth came the passing of one of the great pioneer builders of Iowa Falls and northern Iowa.

☆   ☆   ☆

TWO $5,000 DESKS

Along about 1905 it began to dawn upon me that there might be a possibility sometime of my buying my opposition newspaper, the Iowa Falls *Sentinel,* closing it up, and getting rid of the annoyance. My principal method of attack was upon my competitor's subscription list. According to my theory of newspapering, the foundation of a newspaper is its subscription list. A house without a foundation is not much of a house, and a newspaper without a subscription list is not much of a newspaper.

Each year, for thirty years, I hammered away, with everlasting persistency, at the subscription list of my competitor. Each summer and each fall, I went out or one of my boys went out or some employee went out and combed the highways and byways for new subscribers. Contests and premiums were used. Every time a name was shifted from my contemporary's list to my list there was rejoicing. It was great sport. Eventually, my list of subscribers increased to around 3,600 and my competitor's list went down to around 1,200.

146

Along about 1927 there was little left of my opposition newspaper except a shell and I undertook the task of closing up the institution. Newspaper business was good and I had assembled a good bank account for the purposes at hand. I paid my competitor $12,500 in cold cash for his newspaper equipment and subscription list. After taking out duplications, I added around 400 names to my subscription list, giving me a list of around 4,000.

The Iowa Falls *Sentinel,* the oldest newspaper in Hardin County, was no more, and the Hardin County *Citizen,* for which I had toiled incessantly for over thirty years, was without a contemporary. The death of the *Sentinel* was not without some pangs of pain. This paper came into life at Eldora, Iowa, in the late 1850s, was moved to Iowa Falls in Civil War days, and chronicled the early-day life of the first settlers of the primitive prairies and woods. No other newspaper in Hardin County and few in the state of Iowa told the story of those first years. The files were of great value. The *Sentinel* was a historic institution, the departure of which was deeply regretted by many old-time families and even by myself, although I had labored so long to accomplish this end.

This was to be the supreme moment of my life. This was to be a day of great rejoicing. This was to be a time of standing on the heights of supreme business success. However, as I stood there on the imaginary heights, looking about me, the mirage disappeared. There was nothing there but a vacuum. The joy had been in the pursuit. Out of the $12,500 paid for the property, I salvaged around $2,500 and two office desks.

For my years of labor and my money, I had a net return of two desks, each costing $5,000, just two desks, with glass tops, drawers, and a typewriter stand. At one of these desks, I sit, as I hammer out these words on the typewriter. The other desk is a common piece of furniture in the Iowa Falls *Citizen* office. Strange hands and faces work about it, little realizing the toil and sorrow and hopes and ambitions and cost that cling about this humble piece of office equipment. How many dreams of life vanish with the attainment!

FROM STEAM TO DIESEL

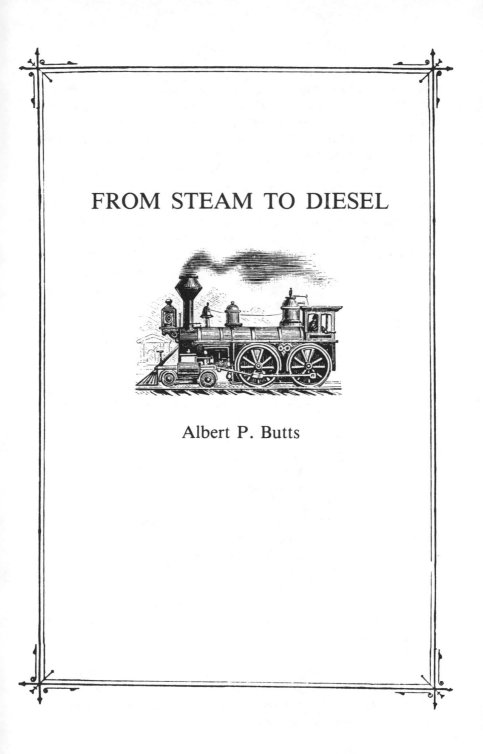

Albert P. Butts

THE COVERED WAGONS *had barely gone out of sight when
railroads began to push out across the prairies. They "opened
up" the country, reaching their zenith during the first half of
this century before cars, trucks, paved roads, and airplanes
began to push them into bankruptcy, and the rails, laid at such
great cost in grueling labor, began to be abandoned.*

*Many persons participated in the romance of railroading.
But few recall it so well and tell it so interestingly as Albert
Parks Butts of Fort Dodge. In 1957 Butts retired from a near
half-century of railroading. He turned to his typewriter during
his seventies and eighties and recorded, for the benefit par-
ticularly of his family, a multitude of his own remarkable
recollections as well as stories passed down from previous
generations.*

*The output of this retired railroader has been little short of
amazing. For purposes of this book Butts loaned an original
manuscript running to more than 260 pages. In addition,
however, came copies of a half-dozen shorter pieces, running
perhaps as much as 50 pages, all typed by his own hand.*

*Many of Butts's experiences resulted from his long years as
a conductor on the interurban, a means of transportation that
is now barely remembered. At one time this electric-powered
means of rail transportation tied all of central Iowa together,
with lines extending 100 miles or more in many directions and
with trains running every hour or two.*

*Butts observed not only the countryside and its develop-
ment and rapid changes but also the cross section of mid-
America with whom he came in contact—immigrants, peddlers,
"boomers," politicians, gamblers, youngsters who rode the
interurban to school, boys going off to the nation's various
wars. He was a keen observer and the laughs, the tears, the
tragedies come through vividly and clearly.*

*Butts began his career with steam locomotives, shifted to
electric (the interurban), and then saw them both replaced with
diesel. He saw it all.*

*Now approaching ninety, Butts lives with his wife in the
typical little white bungalow that would go with retirement and
still sees all these things clearly in his mind. Cataracts have
forced him from the typewriter so he is sharing these excerpts
from the various manuscripts he has written.*

THE BEGINNING AND STEAM ENGINES

Y first railroad work began in 1904 and ended the last of December, 1956. Of the fifty-two years, nearly forty-eight of them were spent on the Fort Dodge, Des Moines and Southern Railway, and forty-three of those forty-eight years were spent as a passenger-conductor. I had the unusual privilege of working with all three forms of motive power: steam, electric, and diesel. Having worked with steam first, it was my first love and the most lasting.

When I first came to Iowa, north central Iowa was just emerging from the pioneer days. My first job was that of a freight brakeman. The Fort Dodge, Des Moines and Southern between Fort Dodge and Des Moines had been built and electrified two years before, but the Newton and North Western between Newton and Rockwell City was still in existence and all freight trains on both lines were operated by steam.

When I hired out I was assigned to the work train. A bulletin was posted asking for a bid for brakeman on No. 79 and No. 80, the local way-freight between Newton and Rockwell City with the Sunday layover at Rockwell City. The distance was 102.5 miles, down one day and back the next. I bid on it and got it. I took my new run, No. 79, north-bound at Boone, August 1, 1909. On August 2, we left Rockwell City on No. 80 at 8:30 A.M. and arrived at Newton at 10:40 P.M., fourteen hours on duty. The next day, August 3, we were called at Newton for 5:30 A.M. with only six hours and fifty minutes rest, and arrived at Rockwell City at 9:30 P.M., sixteen hours on duty. My first week I got in eighty-nine hours which at 19 cents per hour made me $16.91.

In those days before trucks all merchandise was hauled by freight trains. We usually had from three to four merchandise cars, or peddlers as we called them, in addition to our cars of coal, lumber, tile, stock, corn, and oats. The merchandise cars were always carried just ahead of the caboose and were spotted at the depot's long wooden platforms which were at every station. The conductor and rear brakeman, along with the station agent and drayman, and sometimes the town loafers who hung around the depot, would unload the merchandise while the head brakeman was doing the station switching which consisted of setting out loads and spotting empties at the elevator for grain loading and stock cars for stock loading.

The merchandise consisted of everything used by the people in the towns and nearby farms. Dozens and dozens of boxes of groceries of all kinds. Small boxes of yeast, toilet soap, and tobacco; large boxes of wearing apparel: boots, shoes, overshoes, suits, dresses, and overcoats. Still larger boxes contained pianos and organs. At that time all boxes from the smallest to the largest were made out of lumber, usually white pine, and would stand rough handling. The really heavy things were not boxes or crated and consisted of wagons, binders, hayrakes, cultivators, breaking plows, spike- and spring-tooth harrows, buggies, surreys, and hardware of all kinds—from kegs of nails to woven wire fence and rolls of barbed wire—to mention only a few such things. The things we loaded at the various stations were cans of cream and coops of poultry of all kinds. Chickens, ducks, geese, turkeys, and even pigeons which at that time were used at trap shoots, instead of the clay birds that are used now. Many times we would pull into Rockwell City with a full carload of five- and ten-gallon cans of cream for the local creamery, and coops of poultry on a car loaded as high as we could stack them.

The coal dock was also located at Fraser which supplied all steam engines passing by with coal. The coal dock was a high structure with half a dozen bins holding various amounts of coal so that when the chute at the bottom of the bin was opened, all coal in the bin would fall into the engine's tender. When the chute was lowered there was no way of stopping the flow of coal until the bin was empty. That was why there were several bins. Number one would hold one ton; number two, two tons; number three, three tons; and so on. The fireman would have to guess as to how much coal he needed to fill the tender and would notify the dock man, who in turn would tell him to spot the tender at bin number three if he wanted three tons of coal. If the foreman was a poor guesser, the excess coal would overflow onto the ground and would have to be cleaned up by the section men who naturally

Veteran railroader Albert P. Butts of Fort Dodge, Iowa, worked with steam, electric, and diesel during his lifetime.

growled at the fireman for making such a mess for them to clean up and put into some coal car.

I was exceedingly happy with my new run, No. 79 and No. 80. While the work was hard at the various stations, we trainmen rested between stations, I loved to sit up in the cupola of the caboose and look at the farms and fields as we slowly jogged along at perhaps thirty miles per hour. We always waved at the farm boys who were shocking oats or doing other farm work along the right-of-way, which work I had been doing only a short year before. It has always been a never-ending wonderment to me as to how things shape up—how one's destiny is molded and shaped by an unseen hand.

WORKING CONDITIONS AND WAGES

The work of firing a locomotive, though hot and tiring, was nevertheless intriguing. While we had many different engines, No. 4345 was supposed to be our regular engine and we (the engineer and I) cared for her like she was our very own. I had to constantly watch the water gauge to see that the water level in the boiler was kept at a certain level and the steam gauge at or near 150 pounds pressure, but I liked it. A fireman's pay at that time was 20 cents per hour and our assignment was for eleven hours per day which made me $2.20 per day. There was no penalty overtime and we worked as long as there was work to do, sometimes fifteen hours per day, but those long-hour days were few and far between, so my checks ran about $56 per month. By the same token my living was cheap. My room and board was $4 per week, my bed was always clean and the meals were most generous—all I could eat, which was a lot back in those young and growing days. The Higley Hotel where I stayed was an old frame building near the tracks and was operated by Pa and Ma Higley. She always packed my noon lunch in one of those old-fashioned dinner pails, oblong like, with a coffee tank nested in the lower part with an upside-down tin cup fitted over the opening in the center of the top. In addition to two large steak or ham sandwiches made with four slices of bread she always included a large piece of raisin or berry pie. Groceries must have been cheap back in those days to feed us railroaders like she did.

For amusement of an evening we would just sit out on the veranda and talk after supper, and the subjects must have been interesting, whatever they were, for we never lacked having something to talk about. The young fellow that roomed next to me, by the name of Cal, was a boilermaker and once in a while we would go to the nickelodeon, a new movie house that had just been started up and which charged a nickel for admittance. The movies were all silent then. The shows were crude indeed compared to what we have now and the film was run too fast as all the actors seemed to be in a great hurry and the projector flickered badly, in fact when some of the boys spoke of going to the show they spoke of going to the "flickers."

It was here at Hillsdale one night that I saw my first electric headlight. The roundhouse foreman claimed it was so powerful that one could read a newspaper three blocks away. It had two carbons about a half-inch in diameter each, supplied by current from a little dynamo on top of the boiler. When the dynamo was started, the carbons, one above the other with a gap between them, would start arcing and give off a powerful white light. In fact it worked on the same principle as the early street lights.

I have only in a very brief way given you a glimpse of the highlights of my firing days while at Hillsdale. The days were so exciting that I could hardly wait for tomorrow. Of course, I liked the 20 cents an hour I was getting, which was standard for brakemen and firemen at that time. The work was so satisfying and exciting that I really believe I would have worked for nothing, as did many boys along the road who would come down to the depot when we pulled in and help us unload tons and tons of merchandise and help with the station switching just to be around a train. Just to go down to the roundhouse in the morning and get your engine out all cleaned and coaled and make it move to your every beck and call (with a slight movement of the hand it would go forward, stop, or back up) made one have a feeling of power to be able to make those huge pieces of machinery perform. You were doing something almost every minute; you were thinking or figuring how many cars shall I hang onto when I pick up this car of corn to have it next to the others that would be set out on the transfer, or trying to do as little switching as possible with an emigrant car containing horses, cows, farm machinery, and perhaps the emigrant himself who would be in the car to care for the livestock. Many such cars were handled at that time to almost any station on the road. Farmers in Illinois had sold their land at a good price and were migrating to Iowa where they could get as good or better land for half as much. When one tied up at the end of the run, one could look back over the day's work and see

something worthwhile accomplished, something done. One had served the patrons of the road well and faithfully, and like the Village Smithy, had earned a night's repose.

PILE DRIVING AND BRIDGE BUILDING

The several weeks I handled the pile driver in July and August, 1910, were probably the most enjoyable of any equal time I ever spent in my forty-eight years on the road. It was really more like a picnic than work. It was a great adventure for all of us. We had work orders with rights over all trains up to a certain time which meant we could come and go any place at any time on the entire branch. Any time we needed water we would cut and run for it. Any material left at any town that we needed we would simply go and get. If the cook needed groceries any time we would take him into some town and get them. In other words we were as free as a bunch of Indians to come and go and we did so whenever

Steam came first; then electric in the form of the interurban; then diesel. This was one of the earliest steam locomotives in Iowa.

we wanted to. Of course the company expected us to do a good day's work for the hours we put in and we did because we worked with enthusiasm. Some days we would drive six piling and another day twelve.

The bridge gang consisted of only seven or eight men. Dick Foes was the cook. He always had a variety and plenty of it. One day it would be roast beef, next day pork chops, another day beefsteak, another day baked ham, another day fried chicken, another day chicken with homemade noodles. He baked his own bread and always had dessert of some kind, pies of various kinds,

156

apple, peach, raisin, cherry, or perhaps peach cobblers, rice or bread puddings, and always plenty of strong black coffee, strong enough to grow hair on your chest as some of the men would say.

For one of these wonderful meals my crew and I were charged 25 cents each.

RUNAWAYS AND ACCIDENTS

When I went to work for the road in 1909 many of the old system cars were "jacks" (cars without air brakes but with a straight pipe running underneath with an air hose at each end), and when we had some of these cars in our train we brakemen would have to ride the top down the hill and use a brake club on the handbrakes on those cars, which was no fun in the wintertime. Even with the handbrakes set, if the engineer was inexperienced on the hill and had used his air unwisely the cars would get away, and we would go thundering down the hill. All we brakemen could do was to lay belly down on the running board and hang on for dear life hoping and praying that they would hold the rails. I have seen some engineers, when their air was used up, reverse their engines to help slow up a runaway and by the time we got to the bottom of the hill and got stopped the eccentric straps would be almost red hot.

Shortly after that they installed hand-operated block signals on the hill that worked like a three-way switch on a stairway, with lights at the top and bottom of the hill and no train, freight or passenger, was supposed to enter the block while it was lit. By this time we were using electric engines exclusively, having sold our last steam engine in 1914, and the company began running the regular freight trains at night. If any runaways occurred there was no damage done and it was hushed up.

Another time when the brakes on engine 8 failed and a switch happened to be wrong at the foot of the hill near the mine, she ran into the enginehouse, a large wooden structure, demolishing it. An old friend of mine who later moved to Fort Dodge was working near the enginehouse at the time and witnessed the crash and saw the building go down in a thunderous roar of broken and splintered timbers. All those near ran to the wreckage expecting to find the crew trapped in the debris but fortunately they had all jumped when they saw the engine was getting away and in a few minutes they came walking down the hill none the worse for the experience except for jangled nerves.

One afternoon we had pulled into the gravel pit to take siding for a passenger car. While there the engineer said the water in the tender was getting low and he would have to run into Fraser for water. We had an old boxcar for a caboose and four coal cars that were almost empty of ties so the conductor said we would just back up to Fraser with the little train instead of cutting off the engine and running for water. As soon as the passenger car passed, we pulled out on the main line to get orders. After the orders were received, he told us that after taking water we would have to take siding for a south-bound freight train that we were to meet at Fraser. Four or five of us were riding on top of the boxcar caboose as we started to back up toward Fraser. We were not going very fast, maybe 15 miles an hour and were talking and not paying attention to anything ahead of us when suddenly the engineer gave a long blast on his whistle and slammed on the brakes. We all looked ahead about the same time and about ten carlengths ahead and coming around a curve toward us was the freight train we were supposed to meet at Fraser. They were just starting around the curve and had seen us about the same time our engineer had seen them and sounded the whistle.

There had been a steep cut made into the hillside when the grade was first made. The top of this cut was 4 or 5 feet below the roof of the car on which we were riding, and 6 or 7 feet away from the track. We had practically stopped. The south-bound freight, although slowed considerably, kept coming so we all jumped from the car roof to the high bank on the up-hill side. It was a wonder some of us were not injured in making the big jump, but none of us were. The south-bound freight did not quite get stopped and bumped into us hard enough to cave in the old draw bar on our boxcar caboose and break the angle cock, causing the train line to lose its air. No other damage was done. The engineer drove a plug into the broken train line and we all backed into Fraser where we were supposed to meet in the first place.

The conductor said that the dispatcher had given the freight running orders to Boone but had forgotten to add the meet with us at Fraser. Everyone seemed to take the near wreck as a big joke. It was all in a day's work on the "Newton" as the road was still called by the old-timers. The dispatcher was a brother-in-law of the general manager so the incident was never mentioned again.

☆   ☆   ☆

*Those whose lives were spent on railroads, like Albert P.
Butts, saw their share of wrecks.* (PHOTO. ANNALS OF IOWA)

———:⊹:⊹:⊱§⊰⊱§⊰:⊹:⊹:———

I know of nothing more interesting and soul satisfying than
to have a ringside seat in the cupola of a caboose behind a string
of freight cars high above the rails facing the great stage of nature
with its God-made scenery of growing crops, waving grasses,
colorful flowers and leafy trees and the many actors, not trying to
portray some man-thought drama, but real honest-to-goodness
actors playing for keeps on this beautiful stage the real drama of
life.

The prairie country was beautiful. Here and there over the
flat, treeless countryside could be seen a young grove of soft
maple, willows, and cottonwood planted around farm buildings
as a windbreak and protection from the fierce blizzards sweeping
down from the northland in the wintertime. These young groves
also afforded cooling shade for the horses and cattle in the blister-
ing heat of the summertime.

The large areas of swamplands that bordered the tracks were
dotted by hundreds of muskrat houses. In the open water
countless waterfowl swam silently and peacefully about. The
mallards were shallow-water ducks and could be observed duck-
ing their heads under water and diving sufficiently to feed on the
succulent water plants, their tails high in the air. There were ducks
of all kinds and sizes from the little Teal and Butterballs up to
Brant. On their northward flights many remained and nested, like
the beautiful blue-winged Teal, puddle ducks, and mud hens,
which could be seen all summer.

Hundreds of acres of virgin prairie covered by waving
bluestem and prairie grass also bordered the tracks patiently
waiting the farmer's plow to cut their tough roots and turn them
over exposing the rich black soil beneath. This prairie sod was
usually planted to flax after the first plowing as flax was supposed
to rot the tough sod quicker than any other crop.

Dredge ditches were just being dug so tile could be laid later to drain the swamplands. Blair's Lake was the largest of the sloughs along our tracks and was about 3 miles north of Harcourt. It stretched eastward as far as eye could see, and having much open water was one of the best duck hunting sloughs in the county. There were many hunting shacks along its northern edge owned by well-to-do sportsmen, some from Fort Dodge.

On the Rockwell City line many sloughs both large and small bordered the tracks. Two were real large. One southeast of Gowrie was called "19 slough." It was over a mile long and with its cattails, bullrushes and open water was a duck hunter's paradise. On Sundays the hunters would come from as far away as Boone and Fort Dodge, spend the entire day there and catch the last car home. They always had a good bag of ducks. The local farm boys that hunted there told me that "19" was very treacherous and if you got out too far you would sink in out of sight in the muck and quicksand. Their parents probably told them that as a safety measure but on account of their fear they lost many ducks that fell too far out to be retrieved safely.

Having cut my eyeteeth on the steam engines, figuratively speaking, but seeing their end on our road which was being completely electrified, I with several of the steam men decided to transfer into the electric service, so it was in October, 1911, that I took the Rockwell City passenger run and held it until it was discontinued in 1925 at which time I moved to Fort Dodge and took a run out of there and held it until the service was discontinued in 1954 at which time the road was dieselized. Then I took the Webster City–Lehigh freight run and remained on it until my retirement the last of December, 1956.

THE INTERURBAN

The Electric Interurban Railway came into existence from a demand for such a service in the mud-road days. The tracks crisscrossed the country in almost every direction. It gave a service from the rural communities and small towns into the larger cities and it lived a very useful and prosperous life for about twenty-five years and was replaced by the automobile and hard-surfaced roads, just as the stagecoach was replaced by the railroads.

On December 24, 1910, the first interurban passenger car arrived in Rockwell City and beginning on that date two-hour passenger service was inaugurated between Rockwell City and Fort Dodge Junction (later named Hope). The first car left

Rockwell City at 7:00 A.M. arriving at Hope at 7:55 A.M. where it met two mainline cars, one from Fort Dodge and one from Des Moines whose passengers for Rockwell City and intermediate points would change to the Rockwell City car which would leave at 8:05 A.M. arriving back at Rockwell City at 8:55 A.M. The passengers from the Rockwell City branch would change at Hope, Fort Dodge, Boone, Ames, Des Moines, and intermediate points. The passenger cars would continue on this two-hour schedule leaving Rockwell City on the odd hour and continue until 7:00 P.M. with the last car leaving Hope at 8:00 P.M. and arriving back at Rockwell City at 8:55 P.M. where it would tie up for the night.

This fast and frequent service was the greatest thing that ever happened to the farmers along the road up to that time because the cars would stop at any section line or road to pick up or let off passengers. In bad weather a farmer could catch a car for town, stay a couple of hours and return home. The fare between stations was only 10 cents. It was not only the farmers along the road who took advantage of this wonderful service but people from surrounding towns. They would drive to Rockwell City to catch the car every two hours for any place in the nation. Indeed, it was a godsend to one and all at that time. Children along the line after graduation from country schools would ride the interurban cars to Gowrie or Rockwell City high schools. Many of the grandfathers and grandmothers of today look back with the fondest of memories of those wonderful bygone and never-to-return high school days when they rode the interurban.

Sometimes a farmer would ride into town with a three-gallon bucket of cream in one hand and an empty five-gallon kerosene can in the other and catch the next car home. In the summer when the men were busy in the fields the wife would board the car with a basket of eggs on one arm and a baby on the other with several small children along and you got to know them intimately. They often discussed personal affairs or things nearest their hearts with you which seemed to relieve them because they shared their problems with someone who would listen and was sympathetic.

Electric trains were found to be much cheaper to operate than steam. No water tanks, no coal chutes, no boilermakers, no cinder pits, no hostlers, and on our road no firemen, as the freight engines had a set of controllers and brake levers on each side of the cab so that regardless of which side the work was on the engineer could step from one side to the other in a matter of seconds. The power was generated at a central powerhouse and transmitted over the road by an overhead copper trolley wire suspended about 22 feet above the track by long cross arms which were attached to the top of tall wooden poles spaced 100 feet apart.

This overhead, as it was called, needed constant adjustment and repairs on account of wear. This was done by the line gang which consisted of two classes of men, the linemen who wore the climbing spurs in order to climb the wooden poles and make the necessary repairs and, for each lineman, the helpers or groundmen who would dig the holes for setting the poles, attach insulators or bolts or tools or anything needed by the lineman to a rope which would be drawn up by the lineman working atop the pole. The linemen, on account of the hazards of their work of climbing tall poles and handling hot wires, received the highest hourly rate of pay of any employee on the road and they earned it too, since they had to work in all kinds of weather; the worse the weather the more line trouble. In extreme cold weather, zero and below, the wire would sometimes contract and break and it was at such times they would have to be called any time of night or day to go out and splice the trolley wire.

Electric trains are operated in single or multiple units depending on the traffic. On account of the frequent service on our road our cars were operated as single units except on such special occasions as State Fair or some convention. Then as many as half a dozen would be coupled into a train to handle the passengers. For a while when we ran into the Rock Island station at Des Moines our No. 4 consisted of three cars including the parlor car.

Not only did the new electric railroad furnish fast and frequent transportation to the hundreds of townspeople and farmers along the line, it also provided electric current to light their homes and operate washing machines, cream separators, flat irons, and well pumps. Although the 22,000 volt high tension line had been constructed through Easley (2 miles north of Farnhamville) in November, 1910, it was not until 1914 that an extension was built to Farnhamville bringing electricity from the Fraser powerhouse to Farnhamville to light its streets and homes.

I am proud to have played a part of its history. I was young when I started to work on the railroad. The spirit of adventure was strong in my veins. I was thrilled with my work when I was sailing across the prairies in the large passenger cars and stopping at the small towns and an occasional road crossing to receive or discharge passengers. I loved the hustle and bustle at the ter-

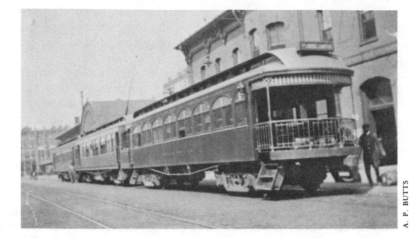

Electric trains—known as interurbans—ran hourly, or even oftener, over much of central Iowa. This train, shown at the Rock Island depot in Des Moines, ran as far as Rockwell City.

minals, the joyous smiles of the people with their hugs and kisses in greeting their dear ones arriving, the handshakes and tears shed for those departing, often farewells for the last time. I hauled hundreds of fine young men, the cream of young manhood, away from their homes and dear ones in World War I and World War II.

SNOWSTORMS

Through the years my motorman and I always prided ourselves on our ability to buck snow regardless of conditions. When reporting to the dispatcher in the morning before our run started, he would usually ask us if we thought we could make it and our answer was always "yes." Sometimes he would tell us that one of the night freight trains had been stuck and had to be shoveled and dragged out.

With us the situation was entirely different. The passenger cars, while not quite as heavy as a freight engine, had twice the speed and in bucking snow it is speed that counts, for the first few hundred feet at least, and most of the cuts were less than 1,000 feet long. In the second place the passenger cars were snappy and quick to respond to the throttle or controller. It is true we would sometimes stall or almost stall and here lay the difference between our ability to buck snow and a freight engine with a string of box cars behind it wallowing through a long drift.

If we could not make it the first time we would back up several hundred yards and sail into the drift at a terrific speed and where we had almost stalled and had left a high wall of snow the impact would be terrific, sometimes knocking a man off his feet, but we in the front end, knowing what was coming, would grab hold of something until the shock was absorbed.

There is no more beautiful sight than plowing snow at night with the powerful headlight making the right-of-way almost as light as day and watching great geysers of the soft fluffy snow flying from the plow like water from a fire hose. We always had plenty of spectators in the baggage compartment at those times because it is an experience one can get in no other way.

Probably the worst blockade the road ever experienced was in February, 1936. We had had over thirty days of continuously below-zero weather and some time in the first week of February it began to snow. On February 7 we had made our turnaround trip to Boone in the forenoon and found the going tough. When we left Fort Dodge on our 4:00 P.M. run it was bitter cold, and getting colder every minute.

The air was full of blowing snow. The storm increased in intensity. Several times we were stuck in drifts but managed to back out each time and finally buck through with the result that we arrived in Boone more than a half hour late. By this time the storm had become so severe that our Superintendent decided not to take a chance on our handling any passengers and getting them stuck in a snowbank all night. He notified all passengers accordingly and gave us orders to return to Fort Dodge light, thinking, as we did, that we had made it down and with good luck we might make it back. We filled our coal box with hard coal and piled an extra eight or ten buckets on the floor which later proved very fortunate for us.

We had no difficulty down through the river valley hill but from there on we were out on the open prairie where the wind got a good sweep at the track and at us. The air was so full of flying snow we could only see about 100 feet ahead of us even with our powerful headlight. By the time we got to Harcourt the Operator informed us that the East Fort Dodge yard was snowbound and the Superintendent decided not to take a chance on our getting stuck. He gave us a message to tie up at Harcourt for the night.

I don't believe I ever put in a more miserable night in my life. We did however manage to keep the car comfortable by continually stoking the hard-coal stove and its humming blower seemed to keep us company.

We got very little sleep, dozing only a few minutes at a time. The blizzard outside was terrible to listen to. The wind blew and shrieked and howled, the car rocked and swayed as if some giant invisible hand was reaching out of the darkness and madly grasping it and lifting it off the track. The wind-driven snow beat against the car windows with all the wild fury the elements could unleash.

By daylight the wind had blown itself out and had calmed and the morning broke clear and cold as usual after such violent storms. The snowplow arrived a little before 9:00 A.M. and consisted of the large wedge plow, engine 209, our largest and most powerful electric engine, and a caboose with the train crew and a dozen section men for snow shoveling.

We followed the snowplow. When we arrived one mile south of Summit we remained to see how the plow would make the cut at Summit. It didn't. The condition was almost unbelievable. This cut, starting at the prairie on a downgrade and curving to the east for 2,300 feet, was filled at places with snow to a depth of 12 to 15 feet or almost level full.

The 209 would back up half a mile and make a run as fast as she could and plunge the plow into the deep drift. It was so deep there was no place for the snow to go except straight up and of course outward. The plow would be wedged so tightly and there would be so much snow under the engine she could not be budged. The 209 would have to uncouple and back away and the snow shovelers would clear the rails by tossing the snow to a man above them who in turn would toss it to the top of the drift. Then the 209 would jerk the plow loose and back up for another run. With all their power and weight 100 feet is the best they could do each time they slammed into it.

It was really something to see and experience. After backing up half a mile for a run they would be going full speed when they hit the drift. It was almost like hitting a stone wall; the snow did absorb the shock to some extent but within 100 feet they would be brought to a stop by being wedged tightly in. How the equipment stood it is more than I will ever know for the punishment was terrible. The 209 was different than any of our other engines and was the most rugged and heaviest built electric engine I have ever seen.

It was the middle of the afternoon before the track was cleared and when we entered the cut it was like going through a tunnel. Many places in the 2,300 feet one could step off the roof of the passenger car onto the top of the drift.

MOONSHINING

Many things happened on the hill other than exciting runaways but I will mention only one. It happened in the prohibition and depression days of the 1920s when the mines were closed and many men were out of work who had families of small, undernourished children without shoes and proper clothing. Rather than see their children suffer they sometimes took chances and did things against man-made laws. The hill was about as sheltered and remote a place as anywhere along the river, with dark, sheltered branches running back into boxlike canyons.

One or two men made hominy out of corn and a couple of times a week they would take a couple of three-gallon cream pails into Boone and peddle it from door to door to make a little money for necessities. I really hated to charge them the 16 cent fare knowing how hard up they were. Others used this same product for a different and more remunerative purpose. It had been rumored that there were stills up some of the hollows but I had never given the rumors a second thought. The line gang had been doing some work on the hill and one day as we were coasting down the hill with brakes partly set some of the linemen jumped out of the brush along the track and gave us a short flag and by the time we got stopped we had run by them perhaps 200 feet. The rest of the gang followed with their paraphernalia and moseyed down the track to the car and began climbing into the baggage compartment. Some had trouble pulling themselves up, and it was then that I realized they were soused to the gills. Some had catsup bottles, some had pop bottles and some had the bottom of their lunch pails full of the clearest and most potent mountain dew (moonshine) I ever saw, genuine corn liquor, unaged, right out of the five-gallon stone jar, so they said. I asked them where they got it and all they would say was "from a friend of yours," so I did not pursue the subject any further as everyone around Fraser rode the interurban. Few if any had cars at that time and I considered all who rode with me to be my friends and I am sure they were. They did, however, inform me that the moonshiner could see our car every time we went up or down the hill and that the still was in plain sight if I looked in the right place. Try as I did for weeks afterward I was never able to locate it. The operator must have been as skilled in the art of camouflage as he was in the art of distillation for although I never tasted his product, those who did pronounced it the finest ever and much superior to the Templeton Tiger Water that was so popular at that time.

That fall, before the frosts had turned the dense and deep-green foliage of the oaks and maples on the hillsides and the ash and willows along the little creek in the ravine to beautiful shades of reds and golden yellows, I was told that, contrary to other manufacturing industries when their product became so famous and popular on account of high quality, excellent flavor and pristine purity, operations had to cease and the plant dismantled. To this day I have never learned who the owner and operator was, and the old hill has never given up its secret. I am sure it had many, for it was here in some of these ravines that the horse thieves of the early days hid their horses. It was also here that one of my engineers while squirrel hunting as a boy in the nineties found a freshly dug grave he was afraid to mention for years afterwards.

SPECIAL RIDERS

When I entered passenger service in 1911 I entered an entirely different world. I literally rubbed elbows with every class of society for those were the mud-road days and everyone who traveled had to ride the trains. The old and the young, the rich and the poor, the great and the humble, the good and the bad, the saints and the sinners. Some of the latter were so vicious they had to be restrained with chains attached to handcuffs and a heavy leather belt as they were being taken to places of confinement. Such cases were always an attraction to the rural and small-town folks who were riding. They would make frequent trips to the water-cooler for an excuse to observe the victim, usually chained to the arm of the seat.

When the women's reformatory was first built on land adjoining our tracks most of the inmates were brought in on our road. I have seen women as beautiful and silk clad and diamond bedecked as a Hollywood star accompanied by some sheriff as well as a lady deputy brought in. I saw also the dregs of humanity with sin-lined faces, cast-down eyes, woebegone and hangdog looks, and wondered what brought them there.

I will start with the many well-groomed and well-fed traveling men who wore huge gold watch chains across their vests from which hung large, solid-gold emblematic charms, some bearing a cross and crown, some double-headed eagles, some a large ivory tooth, all of which they were exceedingly proud and which denoted high rank in their fraternities.

They were men of distinction and honor in their home communities as well as on the road and were looked up to and respected. They carried expensive and highly polished luggage, smoked only the best Havana cigars, and those that drank, drank only the finest and mellowest of whiskies which they graciously offered to share with those around them. They had large expense accounts and when away from home stayed only in the best hotels. They were salesmen of the highest order, not mere order-takers. Most were suave and dignified, with courtly manners. Many had the eloquence, poise, and vocabulary of a Webster or a Patrick Henry and could talk a customer into buying a carload of their products when he probably needed only a gross. They sold everything from buggy whips to threshing machines, everything consumed or used.

Monday morning they would start out on their territory or block as it was sometimes called. The grocerymen were probably the most numerous. Fort Dodge had two wholesale grocery houses, Des Moines three or four, Estherville one. Then there were the meatmen for every packinghouse within several hundred miles, the fruit men (banana men they were jokingly called), the hardware men, the drug men, the farm machinery men, the leather and harness men, the blacksmith men, the tobacco men, the coal men and even the railroad traveling freight agents and traveling passenger agents who would call at prospects' homes and sell them tickets to anywhere from Maine to California and from up in Canada to down in Mexico. These are a few that readily come to mind.

The "drummers," as we called the traveling men from the large cities in the East, sold coats and overcoats, ladies' suits and dresses, millinery goods, shoes and footwear, carpets, jewelry, and watches, to name a few of these. Some carried from two to seven huge trunks and up to a dozen sample cases. They only made this territory two or three times a year and the motormen thought that was too much as they had to wrestle the huge trunks on the car and pile them to the ceiling at times only to have them unloaded at the next station.

PEDDLERS

Among others who rode with me in the early days were the so-called "peddlers." They were a product of the horse-and-buggy days, the mud-road days when the little country towns were young and their stores did not carry a very great assortment of household goods. The peddlers only existed for a couple of generations. Most that I knew came from Lebanon or Syria.

My! how we would like to have the peddlers call at our house when we were on the farm [in Indiana] around the turn of the century. We would look forward to their coming almost but not quite as much as the coming of the Fourth of July or Thanksgiving day. When we would see a man with a couple of heavy packs trudging slowly down the dusty road my sister or I would run to mother with shouts of joy, "The peddler is coming! The peddler is coming!" Mother would be as excited as we were and would go to the front window and pull the curtain aside just enough to peek out of the side of the window with us children close beside her.

When he would mount the front porch steps with his heavy packs one would think he was tired to exhaustion and was hardly able to lift one foot ahead of the other. This would arouse mother's sympathy and she would say, "He looks so tired and weary," which he probably was. He would put his heavy packs down on the porch floor and give a gentle, hesitant knock on the front door. Mother would open the door with a surprised look on her face like she did not know we were having company and he would bow politely and announce with his foreign accent, "Dry goods, Notions," after which she would invite him in, and without any preliminaries he would unstrap the two heavy straps that went around his large telescope valise and lift the top off. Then he would open up the other pack which was a large boxlike affair with drawers that would pull out, displaying all sorts of things like the five and ten cent stores carried originally.

How our eyes would bulge with wonder and excitement at the various items displayed. There were needles and pins, combs, brushes and mirrors, Jew's harps and harmonicas (that we called mouth organs), pocket knives, razors, scissors, cards of various

*Interurbans were for freight as well as passengers. This was at
Hope, Iowa, in 1913.*

sizes of safety pins, gaudy knee garters for the ladies, sleeve
holders for the men, beads, necklaces, and finger rings. Then
from the big valise he would display socks, gloves, stockings,
suspenders, large red and blue bandanas for the men, dainty lace
embroidered handkerchiefs for the ladies, towels, pillowcases,
sheets, gaudy bedspreads, and undergarments for the ladies and
girls. Mother never purchased these because she always used flour
sacks for such garments.

Mother always had a soft spot in her heart for the tired-look-
ing and hard-working peddlers and whenever they would ask to
stay overnight she never refused them. She would go all out to
give them the best of meals.

In addition to our living room we had a parlor off to the
south of it with a nice red ingrain carpet and the usual furniture
consisting of a sofa, several chairs, and the organ. Off this parlor
was the downstairs spare bedroom with a bed, dresser, chair, and
commode upon which sat a large white stoneware washbowl and
huge pitcher that would hold over a gallon of water. On the floor

beside the commode sat a white stoneware combinet with cover, instead of the usual bed chamber. This was as nice a bedroom as any hotel back in those days and was used only for company, and of course the peddlers were considered company so they were always given that room as it was very private. Sometimes dad growled about giving them our best bedroom and treating them like "royalty." He said give them a horse blanket or two and let them sleep on the hay in the barn, which of course he did not mean but only said to aggravate mother; but mother with her true inborn southern hospitality would say, "Now you know you would do no such thing, they are strangers in a strange land and far from home, let us show them what a good and friendly country America is." The pay for such meals and bed was usually a nice handtowel along with a smiling, "Thank you, I will see you again on my next trip."

When I entered passenger service in 1911 a similar group of peddlers was working here in Iowa and rode with me occasionally. In addition to those from Lebanon and Syria some were from Armenia and Russia. They also were rugged men; they had to be to carry the two big telescope valises packed to the top with the various items they were peddling. They headquartered in some of the larger cities where they were supplied by a wholesaler with their merchandise and from where they would start out on Monday morning with their two heavy packs. They would get off at some rural road crossing and start walking from farmhome to farmhome displaying their merchandise and making their sales for cash only. Their meals and lodging were also obtained from the farmers whenever nightfall overtook them and they were paid for in merchandise.

Of course, the peddlers in Iowa, the same as in Indiana, were more numerous in the mud-road days before the advent of the Model T Ford. I knew two who had rigs (horse and buggies) but the rest traveled on foot. As I mentioned, they started out on Monday morning and would get off at some predetermined road-crossing and start their selling. Whenever they were near the interurban they always took advantage of it to save walking. Sometimes when they flagged the car at some road-crossing they would be so weary I would have to assist them up the steps with their heavy packs. They could ride as much as 5 miles for a dime. This would save them a lot of sole leather. Even if they only rode a couple of miles it would save them an hour of back-breaking work. Whenever they rode only a couple of miles they always stood on the platform with their packs. On weekends they would get on the car with empty or nearly empty packs and go into the city to get stocked up again to make a new territory. One fellow who had his young son come over from the old country would take him with him occasionally when he was not in school. He was very bright and eager to learn our ways.

Another who had a rig would leave it at a certain farmhome on the Rockwell City branch on weekends and when he would come back on Monday mornings he would be loaded down with bundles and packages of all kinds and sizes, which I would help him unload. Most everyone on the branch called him by his first name (they probably never knew his last name). He never married and accumulated enough money through his many years of peddling to buy a couple of farms after which he retired. I would often meet him on the street and visit with him for a few minutes about the old days. All the peddlers I knew in later years were keen businessmen.

BOOMERS

In those days, hundreds and perhaps thousands of trainmen were roaming the country, traveling hither and yon just to see the country and be on the move, working only long enough on one road to make a "stake" as they called it and then move on. Most of them were rough, tough, hard drinkers. They called themselves "boomers" and were proud of the name.

They carried "traveling cards" which were really nothing more than an identification card signed by the President of the Order stating that the holder was a member in good standing, and any courtesy extended to him would be greatly appreciated. The boomers were a bold bunch and I think it was they who constructed or interpreted the word "courtesy" to mean free rides. These traveling cards were the same size as the annual passes used on all railroads. The boomer would board a passenger train, find a good seat, and when the conductor came around to collect fares he would hand the conductor the traveling card as though it was an annual pass. If the conductor was a "good guy" he would look at the card like he was looking at a pass, and if he wanted to honor it he would hand it back to the boomer and move on to the next passenger. Seldom a word was spoken. If any questions were asked, the boomers always had a routine reply: they were "looking for work." Once in a great while one would hear of a conductor who would not honor a traveling card and would request a ticket. The poor boomer would then have to dig down in his pocket and pay a cash fare from the stake he had made on a previous job. Information was then spread far and wide that Conductor Jones out of Omaha on the Union Pacific was a dirty, stinking SOB fit to burn in the hottest fires of hell.

Regardless of how good the working conditions on the road were, and the many friends they had made, usually one, or not to exceed two, months was long enough to stay on any one road. Some would stay only a couple of weeks when their feet would get itchy to be going. After collecting their regular check they would be moving on to greener pastures.

Before leaving, they usually asked for and were given a service letter from the Superintendent. These letters were always short and stated in as few words as possible whether the bearer's work was good or satisfactory. Some of the boomers who had been in serious trouble on former jobs and had been fired for good and sufficient reasons, had trouble getting a service letter.

While I have never seen any of these service letters, I have been told that the paper upon which they were written was watermarked with a gooseneck. If the neck and head was pointed upward, well and good, hire the man if in need of help. However, if the gooseneck pointed downward, the man was dangerous and unreliable; do not hire him under any condition.

Don't get the idea that all boomers were evil men or crooks. Far from it. Many were fine men and, far from being dullards or stupid, were well educated with sharp minds. Some were brilliant with splendid vocabularies who would be at ease and fit in with any group of teachers, lawyers, or doctors. Some had razor-sharp minds and some had minds like a sponge that could soak up anything they read. These men could read an agent's switch list with a dozen or more complicated moves, put the switch list in their pocket and switch for half an hour without a single mistake and with all cars in proper place on various tracks or in their train.

They were a gregarious and romantic bunch and on account of their many and varied experiences in faraway places, they were never without a good story to tell, and some on account of their good vocabularies were excellent storytellers.

Their most thrilling experiences were in the mountains. They talked much of their runaways on the steep grades of Sherman Pass or Ratoon Pass when the brake shoes would become red hot from severe braking, or of a trip across the Mohave Desert when something would go wrong and they would almost perish from the intense heat.

Another trait I observed in the boomers in those days was their thinking that all railroad men, meaning of course, trainmen, should travel from job to job and see the country as they were doing. They evidently thought that because they liked that kind of life, all others should. They even had a name for those of us who stayed in one place. They called us "home guards," and were not remiss in calling us that name face-to-face. Although I never heard a boomer criticize a home guard for being such, often when none were around they would speak in a derogatory way about them and belittle them.

SPECIAL TRAINS

Whenever the various transcontinental railroads learned that a large shipment of valuable silk was en route from the Orient to some of our west coast ports destined for New York, their highest traffic officials would vie with each other in fierce competition to handle the trainload shipment across the country, each promising to make the fastest time.

The rate on silk must have been exceedingly high to warrant the elaborate preparations and precautions taken. Among the trainmen there seemed to be an air of secrecy surrounding the movement of such a train. First it would be rumored there was to be such a train, next the sand-house talk would be that the Lake Shore was dickering to get it from Chicago to Cleveland, nothing definite we would understand, just possible. I suppose the utmost secrecy was necessary to forestall or prevent a holdup or wrecking of the train since its valuable cargo would be as tempting as a gold shipment to a bunch of bandits who would stop at nothing to accomplish their purpose, even murder.

These once-or-twice-a-year silk trains consisted of six or seven express cars and in order to make the fast time they were expected to make, they would run nonstop from coast to coast except for engine change and coal and water. They also had the right of track over all trains; even the crack passenger trains would have to take siding for them as they roared by in a cloud of dust, red-hot cinders spewing heavenward from the smokestack and the whistle screaming like a banshee. We trainmen stood far in the clear and marveled at such an exhibition of power and speed. We were all proud of the fact that our road had caught the silk train;

it gave us prestige and something to talk about for weeks afterward: the fast run that Billie Shaw made over the division with that valuable train.

When the President's special was to run, an engineer would be chosen not for speed but for safety and soft handling of the train. He was referred to as a kid-glove man who had the ability to start a train without those on board knowing they were moving.

TAKING THE KIDS TO AMES

When school began in the fall, students began arriving in Ames by the hundreds from all over the country and a greater part of them were funneled over our road into Campus Station filling our cars first to capacity and then to overflowing. At times extra cars would have to be added to handle the crowds. It was their baggage that posed a larger problem. In addition to their clothing for the year and their personal room furnishings the students would bring one or two trunks, one of which would be an upright wardrobe type and the other a large, flat-topped one. These trunks came in such volume and took up so much room on the regular trains with their small baggage rooms that extra baggage cars would have to be put into service. I have seen the Campus Station platform piled so full of these huge trunks and suitcases that there was scarcely room for passengers arriving and departing.

Horse-drawn drays would stand in line waiting their turn at the platform to pick up this baggage. The disposition of these hundreds of trunks must have been a slow process as the different trunks had to be identified by their baggage checks and then taken to the various halls and boarding places.

WORLD WAR I

Those terrible war years of 1917 and 1918 are unforgettable. Our finest and best young men were taken first. I hauled them away by the hundreds. Most of our local boys were taken to Camp Dodge a few miles northwest of Des Moines; it was a crude place.

One young man who had worked on the farm for my father-in-law was a long-time friend. He invited my father-in-law and me to visit him and have "chow" with him (as he called their meals). We took the early car for Des Moines. There was no interurban leaving immediately for the camp so we contacted a taximan. He

For the better part of two decades, around the turn of the century, students coming to Iowa State College could take the Dinkey from downtown Ames to the campus. This depot, moved and remodeled, is now the Hub.

was driving a new Hudson Super Six, a popular and speedy car in those days and offered to take both of us out for $1.25 so we took him up. The taxi let us out at the main gate and as we walked inside, we were amazed at the vastness of the camp.

The hustle and bustle around us was like midway at the State Fair. We passed squads and platoons drilling as their sergeants barked out their sharp orders to them. What seemed confusion to us was orderly to them. The unpaved dirt streets with the raw-looking, unpainted, and barnlike buildings on each side seemed endless.

At noon when "chow" was called, the hundred or so boys came in and seated themselves at the various tables in an orderly manner with no rudeness or horseplay. We sat at the end of a table opposite two very distinguished looking ladies from Des Moines who I think were introduced to us as company mothers.

I have since wondered who the two stately, gray-haired company mothers were. Regardless of their station in the society of Des Moines at that time, and it must have been high, because they had dignity and refinement not encountered in the regular run of women, they were not aloof in their manners or the least bit dainty with their eating, but joked with the boys and ate the plain food as voraciously as a hungry farmer's wife would have. There is no question but what their presence with the boys, many of whom were away from home for the first time, was most motherly, and soul satisfying.

I don't know whether all the many companies had company mothers at that time. If not they should have had if for no other reason than their stabilizing influence.

I will not dwell on the many, many things that happened in my work during the war years. There was hardly a day that it was not heartbreaking to see so many young boys, the cream of our young manhood, boarding my car for Camp Dodge with tearful mothers, sisters and sweethearts and prayerful fathers left standing on the station platform waving a loving and sometimes a last farewell. And those left standing were not the only ones that shed a tear, for quite often the farewells were so touching, so poignant with grief that a lump would rise in my throat that would almost choke me. I would have to turn my head to hide a tear when I gave the signal to depart as if it was I personally who was tearing their dear ones from them.

THE BOONE BRIDGE

The always interesting High Bridge, over 150 feet high and almost 900 feet long, that bridges one of the larger ravines running into the river north of Boone is probably one of the most photographed in the entire country. When the original bridge was built in 1902 it was entirely of wood, was of trestle construction and said to be the highest of its kind in the country. Wood must have been much cheaper than steel at that time. Trestle construction consists of bents spaced 16 feet apart and the widest one in this bridge was 90 feet wide at the bottom or creek bed gradually

One of the engineering marvels of early railroading in Iowa was the old wooden high bridge over the Des Moines River. A. P. Butts's interurban cars used this bridge in 1912.

Steel replaced wood on the high bridge about the time of World War I.

sloping inward to a width of about 10 feet wide at the top and each bent was capped with a 12 by 12 inch cap upon which were placed longitudinally six 8 by 18 inch stringers 32 feet long upon which the track ties rested. Each bent rested on oak piling driven about 4 feet apart with 12 by 12 inch caps on the piling which supported the bent. Each bent was stiffened by sway braces running diagonally from top to bottom, all bolted together with ¾ inch bolts of various lengths with heavy cast-iron washers under each bolt head and nut. There were more than fifty bents in this bridge which made it a gigantic structure. After ten years of use with heavy coal-laden trains passing over it, it became rickety and was replaced by the present steel structure in 1913, which rests upon large concrete foundations and will last indefinitely if kept painted. The dismantling operation lasted several months and all timbers were salvaged with no breakage.

A portable sawmill was brought down from the timber country of Minnesota and the entire structure was sawn into hundreds of thousands of feet of 2 by 4's, 2 by 6's and 2 by 8's of which two elevators were built on our road and the rest sold to lumber dealers, leaving only a pile of sawdust as a memory to this once imposing and gigantic structure. One of the pictures of which I am most proud was one which I took in 1912 while it was still in use.

LOVE, MOTHER

Imogene Hamilton

THE HISTORY of the upper great plains is replete with stories of the viciousness of nature unleashed—the dust storms, the tornadoes, and the great winter storms which swept across the prairies with loss of crops, livestock, buildings, and human life.

Insofar as the winter storms are concerned, many stories go back to the blizzards of the last century. But looking back over three-quarters of this century, a month-long Iowa storm in the winter of 1936 stands out clearly in the memories of all who were living and of reasoning age at that time.

The winter of 1936 was the worst in Iowa's history. Beginning on January 18 and running over to February 22, a blanket of cold settled over Iowa which held the temperatures below zero—at their warmest—for days at a time. Headlines would read: MERCURY CLIMBING—TOWARD ZERO. − 8 AT NOON! MERCURY GOES ABOVE ZERO FOR THE FIRST TIME IN A WEEK!

Schools closed. Trains stalled. Traffic was at a standstill even in cities. Towns ran out of coal and even food. Livestock froze and throughout it all one great blizzard raged after another for more than a full month.

At that time Burt and Imogene Hamilton were living on a 270-acre livestock farm in west central Iowa. They were fortunate. The farm they were renting had electricity as well as running water and central heat. Their two children, Alice and Carl, were away at school at Ames. They were alone, but they had neighbors within a quarter of a mile.

So what was life like under those favorable circumstances during this century's worst blizzard? How was it day-by-day or even hour-by-hour as the mails quit running, fuel ran short, water pipes froze, drifts piled 5 and 8 feet high, livestock died and the cold pushed in relentlessly, driving family activity to that center of all winter family life—the kitchen stove oven door?

Fortunately and remarkably there is a near hour-by-hour chronicle of that time in the lives of the Hamiltons. Letter writing was customary then. (Long distance phoning was virtually unheard of; it cost money.) Imogene Hamilton and her daughter and son exchanged letters every single week.

During that month-long period, shut off from so much of the world and still compelled to communicate even when the *mails quit running, Imogene would write snatches—perhaps several times a day—telling of the growing intensity of the storms and their impact on her shut-in world.*

Note the advantage of the old rural telephone system where it was possible to "rubber," in order to keep track of a concern for other people and their welfare and how finally at 4:30 P.M. on Sunday, February 22, she observed, "Such a long dreary day—the first that I have felt as tho near the limit for me." She did not know that was the end of Iowa's worst storm of this century.

Here are portions of those letters. Bracketed comments are editorial additions, obviously not in the original letters.

Friday P.M.

Y dear Alice—don't be alarmed at this being "penned" in this way—I am watching my supper and doing this at the same time—am starting your letter now in hopes that I will get a chance to mail it tomorrow. Pat [the mailman] doesn't come out here anymore. The last three days he has sent our mail out with Bob [Cairns, neighbor living ¼ mile away] and the day before that we didn't get it at all—it is almost as much bother to go to Cairns for it as to go to town. Dad said he would go in tomorrow P.M. and maybe the laundry bags would be there [laundry was sent home once a week] and then he forgot himself and loaded a load of feed on the sled—if he doesn't go I am quite sure Jim [another nearby neighbor] will—he just can't bear to stay at home. His lane to the R.R. is chuck full about as high as the fence but he can get out this way he thinks, he came over with the sled today—it was his turn to get the mail—and then drove down to Loyd's [another neighbor] mailbox. Said he was going to drive out with the truck

183

in the A.M. There hasn't been a car thru on our road for I can't remember when—have had no school since Mon. and I don't see how they can start next Mon.—am not sure they intend to try.

The forecast over the radio at noon was for much colder again tomorrow. The coal shortage is getting serious. We have enough to last a week or 10 days—it is being rationed out in town. Grandma Hamilton is very low & she was so unconcerned about it—was sure there would be plenty by the time she had to have it.

Lottie [another nearby neighbor] is "on the mend" I think, still plenty sick. They let the "special" go day before yesterday—has had a serious time but if she lives & regains the use of her arm she has, undoubtedly, escaped something much worse—her blood was badly diseased. The snow makes it hard for Fred, he can't get his car out on account of snow. He & G. go in town for dinner & G. gets supper & breakfast.

Have finished hooking the rug & am now bent upon finishing that one I started to crochet a couple of years ago—am getting rid of some junk at least & it has helped so much to put in these days when I'm shut in so much.

Have had our supper and the radio is <u>going</u> & Dad will soon be asleep, will leave this till tomorrow.

☆   ☆   ☆

And what a morning—hope you didn't try to get out to your 8 o'clock—think this is the worst storm I ever saw. 21 below here and the wind is blowing and the snow until at times I can't see the sheep shed. Dad just scooped off the back porch—just a path thru it & the steps & came in with the bottom ends of both ears—they stick out beneath his cap—frozen—I can't help but think of your ears and calves. Wish you'd get something to wear on them. The weather man says tomorrow will be worse.

I don't have any hopes of getting this to the P.O. today. The sun is trying hard to shine just now—10:15. The roads that have been cleared will be worse than ever now—I really wish you could see some of the banks—lots of trails go thru fields and every bob sled in the country is in use.

☆   ☆   ☆

IMOGENE HAMILTON

Imogene Hamilton of Jefferson, Iowa, has seen ninety years of Central Iowa's storms—but none like the winter of 1936.

1 P.M.   Just talked to Josie [an aunt who lived in town with Grandma H.] & they have only coal to last until Mon. I don't see why they haven't been trying harder to get some. The storm is getting worse if such a thing is possible—do hope you don't have to get out.

Drew's [an uncle] had a pair of twin lambs come yesterday!!! I am writing by the open oven door—the most comfortable place I can find—cut out a couple of dark aprons before lunch—will work at them this P.M. & going to clean the bird cages first tho. Am planning to put them in one cage next Fri. They won't sing so much & I'll sort of miss that.

4:45 Dad just brot in the rest of the eggs, 44 today but they will drop off in a day or two as they have felt the weather today. The thermometer has stood at 21 below about all day but is down to 25 now—this will be a bad night—are having to baby the water pipe under the kitchen.

☆   ☆   ☆

After supper & dishes are done—I didn't do them at noon—I only mean to do them 2 times per day—usually wash them morning & noon. Helen Cairns [the neighbor girl who was working in town] didn't get home tonite. I heard her phone at supper time & say there had only been 2 customers in from the country all day, she also said that 3 or 4 trucks & 2 cars got stuck in the snow last nite on the Hiway & Albert Bells had to keep 25 people—think probably that is exaggerated some.

Jim scooped the snow out of the gate by his barn coming this way & he sent word via Lily tonite that the snow was 7 ft. deep where he had it cleaned so nicely.

If I don't get a chance to mail this for a week it will be quite good sized—I rather like writing by "fits and starts" this way—it is hard on you to have to decipher it. You don't need to do it all at once.

Church services have been called off tomorrow on account of the weather & to save fuel.

Am sort of low on reading matter—am either going to try your plan of rereading some of the books or get those old Good House-keeping down & go over them again. Am going up first & put blankets on my bed. I wish I knew you were sleeping warm.

☆   ☆   ☆

Sun. 9:45—Maybe you did sleep warm—I hope so but I'm telling you I didn't. Dad went to bed on the cot & I fired & babied pipes until midnight. Then went to bed & left him down stairs to keep up the good work. I just couldn't get warm—he came up at 2:30 & got his nighty & went back with some blankets to finish the night

For four solid weeks during January–February, 1936, one great blizzard after another raged across Iowa leaving many farm homes cut off from mail, fuel, and, many times, food. The winter of 1936 brought the single greatest concentration of continuous snow and below zero temperatures recorded in this century of Iowa history.

—◦◦◦◦◦◦⧓◦◦◦◦◦◦—

on the cot & I just rose up with covers & came down & the davenport was much more comfortable but didn't sleep much.

Dad thinks this letter a joke—says to tell you he started a snow ball down to you yesterday that should be there today. He is completely "stumped" about his chores today—one day of depriving stock of water is bad enough. Today is better than yesterday but is plenty bad yet. 28 below this A.M. & the snow is still on the move. We can see Jim's gate & it is a fright—he has shoveled so much— Dad has refused to do much until it looked more permanent than it has any time yet. There is a drift that he says, and I believe it, is 5 ft. high right in front of the hen house door—you can appreciate that fact can't you?

4:25 and the storm is much worse, hope you won't try to go to Epworth League. Jim's motor got so full of snow it wouldn't run & I've been worrying about their water supply but he finally got it going a bit ago. The pipe won't run at the horse tank today but Dad has hopes that the trouble is in the pipe coming up and has a lot of hot water ready to work on it.

If I can get them to the P.O., am going to send you another blanket—you may not need them but I'll sleep better.

☆　　　☆　　　☆

Mon. 9:40—22 below when we got up but the sun is shining and not much wind. Dad is going to go down after the mail some time today. I know the laundry bags are there but I am not sure I can wash today. Wish I knew whether or not you'd like another blanket.

Just heard Mrs. Oliver Connor is very sick—they are starting with the sled to meet the Dr. There seems to be some travel on the Hiway today—but there has been only one train thru since day light & that an eastbound passenger.

You never got such a letter before—I haven't the nerve to read it over myself and don't blame you if you get tired before you get this far.

Dad has gone now to feed the sheep & then he is going to start to town.

Take care of yourself & keep warm as you can. I'm putting in a pair of mittens & would put in a stocking cap if I had any idea you'd wear it.

Love
Mother

Wed. P.M.

Dear Alice—yes I'm starting another one of those diaries—If you mind too much just pitch this in the wastebasket. If that check that I sent isn't enough—I'm almost sure it won't be—you pay the difference & I'll make it up to you—Dad says to get a "loud"one. He thinks if you get a snow suit the weather will moderate but he got new underwear last Fri. & just see what happened.

Moorhouses just called & said they had a car of coal in. "Inch" ["Inch" Reever, the mayor] sent out a line call last night that they would not let any more out of town—so Dad stopped this P.M. & told O.B. [Moorhouse] that if he didn't let us have some we would be down to board with him by the end of the week. They were looking then for this car to come in.

I'd use a pen—but keep the paper in a magazine here on the kitchen table and just write when I think of something.

Fri. 11:30 A.M.   I didn't seem to be "moved" to add anything to this yesterday & now while I'm waiting for Katie [a canary] to get dry & warm from the first bath she has taken since you gave her one and while my potato is boiling I'll tell you that yesterday Dad could get 1000# of coal so he went over to get Jim's sled on account it has a box on it & ours has only planks. He brot Lily over here & Jim went with him—I told him to arrange his return trip so they would almost have to eat dinner with us. They went home soon after dinner tho as Jim hadn't fed his hens yet. It seemed so good to have some one in. We are lucky to have them for neighbors.

P.M.   Dad has gone out to chore and I've been working a little on that quilt that I've never finished quilting—got my finger all pricked up.

Edith [Cairns] is "ailing." She told me last night that she didn't feel a bit good—a pain in her side & this A.M. Ethel called the Dr. but he was out on a confinement case & he hadn't gotten there yet the middle of the P.M. She & Ethel waded the snow over to Lily's a couple of times lately & that may have caused her trouble.

Drew bought him some ewes last fall to lamb next spring & one of them had twins last week—they died. But they have had 1 set of triplets, 1 twins & 1 single this week & saved all but a triplet that they attempted to raise on a bottle.

Josie got 1000# of coal yesterday, too. We don't have enough to last a week but there is no use worrying about it and we are so much more fortunate than so many others.

☆   ☆   ☆

Sat. A.M.   And more grief—the pipe coming in from the hard water cistern is frozen. Dad is talking of cutting the thing where it comes into the basement & trying to thaw it but my faith is very weak concerning the proceeding.

15 below this morning & looked snowy at first but is beginning to

clear now (10:30). Expect you are at class now. Hope you are going to get your snow suit this P.M. Am so sorry you didn't have one for all this bad weather.

Clyde [another uncle] loaded his eggs & cream in the sled yesterday & started to town to get coal—got a little way on the road & got a horse down in a snow bank & went back home.

There haven't been any trains into Lidderdale & Lanesboro since a week ago yesterday & they are having a hard time to get groceries as well as coal. If everybody had depended on using horses & just kept going instead of trying to dig out for autos it would have been better. The worst place between here & town is the street south of the track. I think Dad plans to walk down with his pipe after a while & I'm going to send this as I am not sure when I'd get another chance. I had hoped to send you some little thing as a valentine but didn't know that I'd have any way to mail it.

Lily just called & said Jim was going downtown with the sled & Dad could go with him.

There is a snow bank on the N side of the feed bunk that lets the calves walk right up into it & it extends right on south clear to the fence going west from the horse barn, Dad, Gyp [family Collie] walk right out over the fence and today a calf has discovered that it can do it too.

Jim & Dad are ready to take off with Dad's pipes.

Sun. 2/22/36 4:30 P.M.   Such a long dreary day—the first that I've felt as tho was near the limit for me. 26 below this A.M. & hasn't been above zero all day. Snowed most of the A.M. & has been cloudy most all day. Bud went to town on horseback to get a Sun. paper—can't go in the road south of our house even that way—it looks from here as tho the snow was about as high as the fence.

Have given up trying to do anything for the frozen pipe until the weather moderates. Think the trouble may be right in the cistern. Had a calf this A.M. that was bloated almost to the bursting point—knew Doc couldn't get here so Dad operated on him—as far as eliminating the superfluous gas was concerned the operation was a success & the calf was still alive at noon. These weather conditions develop pioneer instincts I think.

I wanted to hunt the eggs just to get a breath of fresh air but Dad insisted on doing it so I'll do without the freshness. Wayne has been walking out to Clyde's delivering their mail—froze his face yesterday.

☆   ☆   ☆

Mon. A.M.   12 below & snowing & blowing—most discouraging. Weather man doesn't promise anything better. Jim is going for coal this A.M. & Dad seriously considering going after ours this P.M. instead of waiting until tomorrow—that eliminates a chance of getting the mail tomorrow which really means a lot to me.

Dad just came in & says tell them "I get on a snow bank at the sheep shed & walk right on top of it, over the fences to the feed bunk at the cattle barn & can mount one at the horse tank high as my head & go to the shop." There is nothing to hinder all the stock getting out except their fear of going thru. The fodder hauling is the real job now. I asked him last night if he didn't wish he had no stock—he had to study the matter over but finally decided he would rather have it if he could only take <u>good</u> care of it. There has only been one or two days that it has been hard for him

IMOGENE HAMILTON

to keep from getting too cold. Every time he goes to town he sees
something funny. The last time when they got almost to town they
met Billy Everts walking out with one of those paper shopping
bags like we get at the 10¢ store loaded & when they were starting
home they met "Fat" [Billy's son] walking in. They told of
hearing of a man walking with a scoop shovel on his back.

5:20   Have put my soup to cook. Dad gets thru about 6. He froze
his face quite badly this A.M. He had to haul fodder & a wagon
box of beans to the sheep shed. The wind has been bad all day and
it looks now as tho this would be our coldest night.

Jim brot the mail this A.M. Left it in the box as our snow is too
deep to haul a load of coal thru unless necessary—I was so anxious for the letters that I donned my "snow suit" & went after
them—I didn't get a bit cold but did a lot of floundering around &
seemed to get my breath swallowed. Any how I was about winded
when I got back—was so glad I'd gone when I saw Dad's face.

Tues. A.M.   Most noon. Was 22 below again this morning & sun
shone a little while, snow is beginning to move some now. Dad has
been out for fodder, don't know whether he will go for coal this
P.M. or not. There are 3 cars on the track today & the dealers are
trying to get it unloaded but the roads are so bad that people living
out very far can't get in. I suggested to Dad that he wait until
tomorrow as his face is pretty tender today—there is a bare
chance it might not be so cold tomorrow.

Carl—in regard to attending your banquet [some event on the
campus; Dad and Mother always faithful even in times like
this]—Dad says if the weather is permissible I'd better plan to go
but he doesn't see how he can get away—I hate to go without him
but I don't really see how he can get any one to do the chores.
They are pretty much complicated and will be for some time, so I
believe I'm going to try and go anyway. Just doesn't seem like I
could start into "spring work" without seeing you folks. There is
just one more thing bothering me and that is what kind of a dress!
Please let me know at once.

Mrs. Connor died this A.M. Bertha got home at midnight last
night. A terrible time for a funeral.

MOTHER

UNSEEN BATTLES

Dr. Sylvester W. Barnett

STORIES of "the old country doctor" are legion. Every community had one who became a legend in his own lifetime. They did "general practice"—the surgeon, the internal medicine man, the family counselor, the community's "security blanket." They made house calls for $2.50 when it meant going by horse and buggy through rain and snow and mud. Patients frequently showed their appreciation by paying their bills "in kind"—farm produce; and not infrequently by not paying their bills at all. Many an old family doctor closed his doors with "thousands of dollars on the books."

A few have told their stories—rather privately. One of those was Dr. Sylvester W. Barnett. Practicing medicine was a way of life with Dr. Barnett's family—on both sides of the family—going back several generations. To do anything else was the exception and in Dr. Barnett's little book, Unseen Battles of the Night, he cryptically observes that "Uncle Frank strayed a little; he became a dentist" and "the other brother, when an infant, fell in a well and drowned so he couldn't study medicine."

You see they didn't let them off easily when they didn't study medicine in that family!

And it continues. Dr. Barnett had three children, two sons, Robert M., William H., and a daughter, Marian. The sons are both doctors and the daughter has devoted her life to heading the nursing departments of several large hospitals.

Following are excerpts from Dr. Barnett's 100-page book which recorded his lifetime of medical experiences. It was published in 1974. His 50 years of practice included his stint in World War I. Most of his experiences occurred in the Cedar Falls, Iowa, area.

These excerpts are reprinted with minor changes by permission of the Congdon Printing Company, 203 State Street, Cedar Falls, Iowa, where copies of the complete book may be obtained.

—⊹⇥⊱⊹⧸⊰⊱⊱⧸⊰⊹⇤⊰⊹—

N my office in 1925, a lady brought in her three-month-old baby with diarrhea ("summer complaint"). There was no doctor in Cedar Falls who made feeding formulas or gave instructions about baby feedings. This baby was one of four in the family and was eating everything from soup to nuts. It was dehydrated and had a severe acid diaper rash. It looked sick! I had plenty of time so I sat down with the mother after examining the baby. I made out a formula, learned from Dr. Alt and Dr. Holt at St. Luke's, told her how to make barley water and how to mix the formula, and how to make Farina. I spent about an hour with her. I asked her to bring the baby back in four days. She walked out. That night when I left the office, I found, at the bottom of the stairs, my written instructions and formula. I was surprised and wondered why that was. Then it occurred to me: these people had been trained to take medicine and I had given none. So I waited for the next sick baby. In a few days in came a mother with a sick baby, same way, "summer complaint" due to hot weather. I went through the same speech and gave the same formula. Then I went to the drug room, got a four-ounce bottle, put one ounce of ordinary neutralizing cordial in it, the rest water, put a label on the bottle and explained to the mother, "This medicine must be given after the feeding. Do not give it before the feeding. Follow the schedule I gave you and then give the medicine. Come back in four days." When she returned in four days she brought a lady with her that wanted the same kind of medicine for her baby and the neighbors. So I went through the same speech again and became well known for the feeding and the medicine I gave for diarrhea. Of course the medicine had nothing to do with the recovery. I learned that medicine is sometimes more

195

196

powerful than skill. So now I know what Hippocrates meant when he said, "Medicine sometimes cures, often relieves, but always consoles." That was in 450 B.C. and still is true.

☆   ☆   ☆

PNEUMONIA WAS "CAPTAIN OF THE MEN OF DEATH"

One member of a family would take sick with a chill, cough bloody sputum, have pain in the chest, and high fever. Often the whole family would be sick at one time. These were all home calls, night or day. At one time I had nine cases that had the crisis (turning point) on the same day and each one wanted you there.

When sulfanilamide came out, I went to Iowa City to see the results. The drug was not yet on the market. Dr. Horace M. Korns showed me the cases and records. A bottle of 1,000 sulfanilamide tablets sat on his desk. He was called out of the room for some reason so I grabbed the bottle and poured out a couple of handfuls and put them in my pocket. When he returned, I was calmly reading the state Journal. I went home and a week later was called by the County Supervisor to go to see a sick child. It was double lobar pneumonia. I started the kid on four tablets three times a day. The next morning I couldn't believe what I saw. He was blue as ink (sulfa was a dye) but he was feeling fine and wanted more food to eat. There was still some temperature. The third day I ran out of pills. The kid felt fine but his chest sounded like a chocolate malted milk. I called Dr. Korns and told him I had a severely sick kid with pneumonia. Could he send me some sulfanilamide? He said, "What did you do with the pills you stole?" I told him I had given them to this boy but needed more. He told me sulfanilamide would be on the market the next day. I called E. R. Squibb & Company in Chicago and requested 1,000 tablets at once. They sent them! When I got the bill I thought there was an error. I forget how much it was, but it staggered me. The Supervisors paid for the sulfanilamide used and $10 to me for my services. So pneumonia was feared no more. Then penicillin finished the job. Miracles in the field of medicine.

Diphtheria: that was the baby that really killed! A sore throat or the croup was always diphtheria until proven otherwise. Night and day the calls came; they were answered, a smear was taken and a culture made. A trip to the office or the hospital, the slide stained, and the bacteria identified. The culture was put in the in-

WILLIAM H. BARNETT

Dr. Sylvester W. Barnett, physician in Iowa from 1925 until the 1970s, practiced mostly in the Cedar Falls–Waterloo area.

cubator and, if positive, a trip back to the home and antitoxin given. I often gave antitoxin on suspicion in case of temperature, the croup and a membrane on the throat. Then you sat and waited. In the case of tracheal diphtheria, I often put an emergency tube in the windpipe and stayed or returned in twelve hours to check. Immunization put a stop to all this. I saw the last diphtheria in 1928.

During the days of quarantine the Health Officer ordered a sign put on the house: quarantine for diphtheria and scarlet fever, warning signs for measles (Red or German), whooping cough, mumps, typhoid fever, and meningitis. When I had scarlet fever as a little child, my mother was quarantined in the room with me. A sheet was hung on the inside of the door and kept moist with carbolic acid solution. Everybody stayed out. Mother and I stayed in. We had a thundermug under the bed. It was used with a solution of carbolic acid in it. Dirty linen was placed in a tub under the bed and soaked with carbolic acid solution for two days. In the evening they were placed outside the sheet over the door. My Dad would take them to the bathroom and dispose of the stuff: some down the stool, some in the bathtub to soak for twenty-four hours. After the disease was cured, the doctor had proven this with three successive smears, a day apart negative. Now the patient had a bath which was welcome. Then all clothes were put to soak in the bathtub. The room had two formaldehyde candles sitting in a dish of water. They were lit and the room was sealed for two days. What a stink!

Measles was a necessary evil but often had severe complications followed by tuberculosis. Quarantine was for fourteen days, 90 percent contagious.

German measles: we thought there was nothing to it! We know better now.

The question about chicken pox was is it or is it not smallpox? I recall one man from Milwaukee who walked into my office. He was staying at the Black Hawk Hotel. He was sick and all "busted" out with smallpox. I couldn't put him in the hospital, I couldn't let him travel, so I put him in the detention hospital with a special nurse in attendance and a telephone in his room so he could talk to his family. There he stayed for one full month. Everyone who had contact with him or had been exposed was vaccinated. He was very sick but got well and was very grateful.

I recall two epidemics of meningitis. In one family of three, the mother and daughter were ill. We set up a quarantine in the hospital. I did a spinal puncture on each of them and injected the serum. They both got well. I had about a dozen cases and two died. Sulfadiazine changed that story.

I was in St. Luke's Hospital in Chicago when a shipment of oysters came to Chicago. It was reported there were two thousand who took sick with typhoid fever in one day. Our hospital got about one hundred cases. In private practice I had three cases. One was severely ill with hemorrhages. I transfused him a number of times. This man got well after a long time. He had no money so decorated the interior of our home in gratitude. One bad complication: flat, painful feet from being in bed so long. Typhoid inoculations took care of this disease.

Poliomyelitis was feared by all parents and doctors. Nothing could be done! Then the use of serum taken from those who had had poliomyelitis came as a relief to doctors. I kept some in our icebox where I could grab it. It must be given within the first twenty-four hours of the illness. So again, night or day, the call was answered and blood drained equal to the amount of serum to be given. I used it faithfully and after one year I was convinced that it was the saver. Now we know it was not.

☆   ☆   ☆

The snows of 1936 were terrible. Calls came to the office and to my home. They would say, "Doc, our little girl is awfully sick. Can you come out, we can't get in?" It snowed all winter and was extemely cold, 34 inches of snow on the ground; the temperature was 30 to 35 degrees below zero for days.

A call came in that a lady, 5 miles north towards Janesville, had pneumonia. If I would start, the farmer would meet me at the country schoolhouse with a horse. So I started. I got along slowly until I got to the schoolhouse which was on the corner where you turn to Black Hawk Park. No farmer with a horse. So I went into the schoolhouse, built a fire and waited an hour; still no farmer. So I went out, started my car, and got going. I always carried a shovel, a blowtorch to warm my cold car, a box of sand and two sets of chains. I had tough going shoveling and going as far as possible, then doing it over again. Then I heard the worst racket in the road back of me. I looked and the snow was flying everywhere. This monster came to a stop back of my car. A man got out and said, "What the hell are you doing out here?" I said,

"I came out to see how the chickens were laying. Can't you see that emblem on the back of my car? A woman out here has pneumonia and I'm going to see her." He said, "Why didn't you say so?" He dug a hole in the snow beside the road, pulled my car back out of the drift, and then I backed into the hole. We hooked a chain on the front of my car and started out. We got to the farmhouse where a dish towel was hanging on the gatepost. My car was parked in a hole the plow dug at the side of the road. That was the place! The driver of the plow said, "I'll be back this way in an hour, you wait here and I'll pick you up, you should be turned in to the police." So I plowed on foot to the house. The farmer with the horses was not there yet. The thermometer outside their house registered minus 38 degrees. Maybe so! I went into the kitchen, it was cold, the stove was burning wood and coal but all the stuff in the cupboards was frozen. I left my lambskin coat on, did take my hat off, and went in to see the sick woman. Her temperature was 104½ and she was delirious. She had lobar pneumonia. It was -4 degrees in the bedroom. We moved her into the dining room near the pipeless furnace. Now the husband came in. He never did make it to the schoolhouse and was surprised to see me there. I fixed the medicine, tincture digitalis, phenacetin, Brown's cough mixture, embrocation, and twelve ½ grain tablets of codeine. I said I'd be back tomorrow. However, it was five days later before I made it. She had had her crisis and was fine. Now I went out to my car. No snowplow in sight, so I got my blowtorch going, put it under the cold pan, got the car oil warmed up and started the car. I had on high galoshes, a lambskin coat, gloves and mittens. Still no snowplow, so I started home. I hadn't gone far when I got stuck in a drift. Sure enough, here came the snowplow, the first rotary plow I had ever seen. He stopped, gave me the worst cussing I had ever had, but I didn't talk back. We got to Cedar Falls at First and Franklin Streets. He got out and told me off again. Then he said, "How was the lady?" I said, "Thanks to you, she will be all right." He said, "Don't try that again, I may not come along." The charge for the trip was $2.50 plus $1 a mile one way, or $7.50 plus the medicine. Those people, however, were my friends until they died.

One other call comes to mind. A doctor from Hudson called and said he was at a farmhouse; his patient had an obstruction. Could I bring an ambulance out to get him? I called the two funeral homes in town but both were snowed out some place. It was about 10:00 P.M. so I decided to go out and get the man. I got there Okay. He did have an obstruction and a palpable tumor. I gave him morphine. We wrapped him in a blanket and put him in my car. The doctor from Hudson took the the wife and son and went ahead to break the way. I got along all right until I hit the correction line, where there was a huge snowdrift. I got stuck so I got out and shoveled, then a chain broke. When I took off my mittens to fix the chain, my gloves, which I wore under my mittens, stuck to the chains, and my flashlight burned out. I finally got the chain off.

So I dug my way out of the drift and started for home. I finally made it! My patient was sleeping fine. There in the lobby sat the doctor and his people calmly waiting for me. We got warmed up and went to the operating room. I did a posterior gastroenterostomy.

I could have frozen that night. My skin peeled on the inside of my legs, ears, and both heels. The patient got along okay, but of course died later since he had cancer of the stomach.

☆   ☆   ☆

Once a man came to our door and said his wife was having a baby, could I come. He said he had the money. I didn't want to go but decided the woman needed help. I got my car and followed the man. We went to the house. The man went in and then left. I checked the woman and then sat down to wait.

At 5:00 A.M. the baby was born. I cleaned things up, made the patient comfortable, and asked where her husband was. She didn't know. It was raining hard now. I looked out towards the barn and saw him so I walked out there. He disappeared and hid so I went back to the house. A neighbor lady had come in to help.

I went home, cleaned up and went to the hospital. Two days later I drove out to that place and caught the man unaware of my presence. His wife was fine and also the baby. I asked him where my $25 was. I was sore because she was a nice woman and he had lied to me. He told me he would get the money from the bank. I saw a threshing machine sitting out in the back yard. When I got to town, I called the bank and learned that he had no account and no credit, so I attached the threshing machine. It was sold at a sheriff's sale under someone else's name. The lawyer got $24.00, the Justice of the Peace got $20.00, sheriff's sale, $500.00, signer of the notice, $5.00. I got $6.75, so another lesson was learned. I have never sued for a bill since.

202

In those days there were only a few scattered telephones in the country. They often would be on the same line, the Benson Telephone Company. I went rain or shine, sleet or snow. At night they were to hang a lantern on the gate, in the daytime a dish towel. You would be surprised at how many lanterns or dish towels would be hanging out, especially if an epidemic was taking place.

☆　　　☆　　　☆

One other experience before I go back to the routine practice of medicine. I was always interested in athletics and attended all games when possible, especially high school games. In 1928, it was suggested that I become the team physician for the Cedar Falls High School teams. So I sat on the bench, was the first one on the field or floor when an injury occurred, whether it was friend or foe.

My younger son, Robert, was quarterback of the high school football team. They were undefeated. In one game he was pulled out because he didn't act right. The coach said for me to take a look at him. My son was stubborn and got mad at the "old man." I kept him out the entire second half.

That night I heard him up in his bathroom vomiting. I went to his room, diagnosed an acute appendicitis, and took him to the hospital. I did the appendectomy myself, because it was during World War II and there were no other surgeons on whom I could call for help. The appendix was red hot. He got along fine and was to go home on the eighth day. That afternoon the hospital called and said he had had a chill, severe pain in the abdomen, and his temperature was 104 degrees. I went there at once and called a Waterloo surgeon on consultation. We decided to open him up and see what was going on. We did; only bloody serum was present. A smear was taken and a culture. The smear said streptococcus infection, which was deadly.

Now, what to do for my own son? I had had three cases previously and all had died. I called Dr. Frank Peterson, head of surgery at the University of Iowa, and Dr. Horace Barnes, chairman of the Board of Control at Mayo Clinic. Dr. Barnes sent some of the new drug, penicillin, then being tried out, and so did Dr. Peterson, by car. Nobody knew how much to give. I gave 10,000 units every three hours for seven days. At the end of 48 hours the temperature was normal, pulse normal, drainage decreasing, and the mass, felt rectally, decreasing in size. I reported each day to Dr. Peterson and Dr. Barnes. The medicine was continued for two weeks. Now the boy was well and was able to play basketball. That was the important thing. When I replaced the penicillin they had sent me, after it came on the market, I found it had cost me $10 a shot or $80 per day. My son was worth it and, as Dr. Barnes said, it was "cheaper than an undertaker." I believe he was the first patient in Iowa to receive penicillin, previously exclusively in the hands of the military. This which I had received was for institutional trial and was smuggled to me.

ACCIDENTS AND EMERGENCIES

A boy about eight years of age was brought to the hospital. He had run out into the street chasing a ball and into the path of a car. The handle of the car caught in his mouth and dragged him down the street about 100 yards. When I saw him at the hospital, lying on the table, I was shocked. The entire left side of his face was torn wide open. You could see the muscle and flesh stripped down the left side of the neck. I could see his windpipe, the carotid artery, the jugular vein. He was not bleeding severely and seemed not to be in much pain. I put a suction tube in his mouth and began the reconstruction of his face. I first put steel wire in the two broken ends of the jawbones, both sides, then I put sutures in the floor of his mouth, then in the muscles outside the mouth and throat. I was using local anaesthetic and he was to move his foot if it hurt. Now I began tying the sutures together. First, the jawbones, then the chromic sutures in the mouth, and then the muscles on the outside of the throat. Still no severe bleeding. I knew the mandibular artery was torn and that included the mental artery. I tied them even though they were not bleeding. The mandibular nerve was left unsutured. Now I sewed the skin, all interrupted sutures. We had no antibiotics. He was given tetanus toxoid and put to bed. He could swallow and looked much better with his face sewed closed. However, I knew we had a long way to go. Would the mandibular (jaw) bone grow? Would the tooth buds all die? We got through the first state without infection. He was tube-fed for ten days. Some of the stitches were removed. He could move his mouth, open and shut, but was not allowed to chew. He could not talk yet but could smile with the right side of his face. He was an excellent patient, a real nice boy. By this time I had had a dentist see the boy and X rays taken. He remained in the hospital. The swelling in the face decreased. He could take liquids well and wanted to go home.

The boy was brought to the hospital each week for me to see. He had been turned loose to play and had injured the left side of the face and infection was present. X rays showed he had an osteomyelitis (bone infection) of the mandible. I watched and waited. After some time I took a piece of dead bone out, a little later another and before I was through I had done a bone graft on the mandible from the shinbone. It grew! Now the tooth buds were dying, so Dr. Jensen extracted them. Then more trouble: the top portion of the suture at the vermillion border of the lips was sloughing. I cleaned this up and after a time did a skin graft. After fourteen months a mold was taken of his gum lines and a lower plate made. He now began to look fine. Then another abscess formed and I extracted another piece of dead bone. So it went. After two years he was ready for discharge.

The insurance man came in for settlement. The boy's parents wanted to be paid for the care they had given the boy. I finally reached this agreement with the insurance company: my bill was acceptable and the dental and hospital bills were acceptable. The boy would need new teeth in the future as he grew. I suggested that $1,500 be placed in trust in the First National Bank with the insurance company as cotrustees and the work to be done okayed by me. To my surprise, the insurance company agreed. I knew if the father or mother got the money it would vanish.

Some ten years later a young man walked into my office to see me. It was the boy. He looked fine, very little scar and a perfect jaw, why, I do not know. He went to see the dentist. We were very proud of our job. In those days you couldn't call a specialist. You must do the job yourself and you must proceed and not make a mistake. We had attacked the problem directly—and won.

☆   ☆   ☆

In another automobile accident I was called to Island Park [on the north edge of Cedar Falls]. It was a hot day in August, maybe about 4:00 P.M. I drove out 218 North. Here was a car on the right side of the pavement. Two women were lying on the grass so I supposed they were the victims but someone said, "Here is the man!" I walked around to the other side of the car. Here was a man with a guard rail, a 2 by 8 plank, which had run

through the right car door, through his abdomen, and had pushed
him out of the car. The plank had gone into the open left car door.
I couldn't believe it. I started giving orders: get a saw, call an ambulance, call the hospital and tell them we are coming in (this was
before the days of radio). The guy said, "Get this darned board
out of my belly." He was pretty drunk. We sawed the plank off
on the right side. The plank stuck out so far on the left side that
we couldn't get him in the ambulance, so we sawed some off on
the left side. I had given him a shot of morphine in the back. We
couldn't lay him down on the ambulance cart so we loaded him
semi-sitting with the plank still in place. We went directly to the
operating room and left him on the ambulance cart. I had two
doctors called, one to help me and another to give intravenous
fluids, check the blood pressure, pulse, etc. The patient wanted
only one thing: "Get that damned plank out!"

I cut straight across the abdomen. Door padding, chunks of
shirt, overalls, and dirt were in the abdomen. The plank was un-
threaded through the torn intestine and the destruction surveyed.
There was not much bleeding. Irrigation with salt solution made
the intestinal contents identifiable. The patient was given some
anesthetic. I resected about 7 to 8 feet of the small intestine, two
feet of large intestine, sewed a tear in the liver, controlled all
bleeding, did an end-to-end suturing of the small intestine and the
colon, leaving an opening (colostomy) to the outside, and sewed
the belly up. The guy was in pretty good shape. He was given 500
ccs of whole blood and was taken to bed.

To my surprise, the patient got along fine. He was always
wanting some whiskey which he didn't get, but maybe should
have. About 3:00 A.M. four days later, I was called to the hospital.
All windows were open as there was no air conditioning. I could
hear him screaming when I was a block from the hospital. When I
saw him, both legs were pulseless and white, his abdomen soft,
heartbeat rapid, and the lungs full of rales (moisture). He went
right ahead and died. How he lived that long I do not know. We
posted him: clots had formed in the arteries to both legs, a large
clot had lodged in the lung. What was the cause of death? He was
signed out as pulmonary embolus. Any one of a dozen things
could have killed him. However, we got the plank out and sewed
him up.

☆   ☆   ☆

In another instance, I had a man who went through the windshield, severely lacerated his face and scalp, and cut the right ear off. It was just hanging by the lobe. I looked at his ear. It was dark blue, so I knew the circulation was poor. I laid it back in place and put a moist saline pack on it. I proceeded with the suturing of the other wounds and then looked at the ear again. It was a little pinker. I had never sewed an ear back on but decided to try. All sutures must be put in first, tied last. There is no room back of the ear to sew so I was tying the sutures when an older doctor walked in and said, "You young doctors are crazy, that won't grow." I finished the job and the patient was put to bed. We learned he was from Oklahoma and had no permanent address. He was a very kind and courteous patient. At last the sutures were removed. The ear had grown back. I had learned another lesson: sew it on, you can always cut the ear, finger or whatever off if necessary, later on.

The next morning the man was gone. Nobody was paid. The hospital officials were mad because I should have made him a state case and sent him to University Hospital at Iowa City. Some few years later, a well-dressed man walked into my office and wanted to see me. My time was full but the receptionist let him in to see me. He said, "You don't know me. Look at my right ear." I did. A small defect, a forehead scar, showed and now I knew him. He sat down and we visited. He had struck oil and was wealthy. He wanted to pay his bill! We had put it in the past-due-and-probably-lost-forever accounts and at the moment could not find it. We did later. He decided that the loss of an ear according to insurance was $500, which he insisted on paying me. He then went to the hospital and paid his bill there. The bookkeeper was dumbfounded. There are honest people in this world! I heard from him a couple of times after that and that is the end of that story.

☆　　　☆　　　☆

One got all sorts of calls: One baby I delivered upstairs in a house with a leaking roof, so I wore my raincoat. Another call was for a gypsy woman lying on a dirt floor in a tent. To my surprise, while I was packing my stuff, she got up and started picking up the newspapers on the floor and bossing the kids around. She handed me $30 in gold pieces. She had paid the last doctor $50 and thought it was too much. I drove out that way the next day to see how things were—she was doing the family washing! The husband wanted to give me $10 more because it was the best delivery his wife had ever had.

My office girls estimated that I delivered between 1,600 and 2,000 babies. Maybe so. I delivered eleven pairs of twins and one set of triplets. All the twins are still living I believe. I was working on my second generation when I was forced to stop obstetrics. Home deliveries often consumed a twelve-hour stay, usually all night. Then you would eat some breakfast, get the blowtorch out (if it was in the winter), put it under the car to warm it up, and fight the snow all the way home. All this was over after pavement and snowplows came into use. Some of my worst and hardest trips in the country were to deliver a baby. All by yourself, you prayed and worked at the same time, then rejoiced when the job was done.

☆   ☆   ☆

I recall another lady out in the country. Her doctor had been called out to see her and diagnosed gall bladder disease. He gave her some morphine for the pain. It snowed and he couldn't get out to see her for four or five days. When he did she was in bad shape. He brought her into the hospital by ambulance. As I checked her over after the laboratory work was done, I said to myself, "It's probably a ruptured gall bladder and peritonitis. She will die unless she is operated and probably die if I do operate." We operated. There was bile in the abdomen and loose stones. I picked out all I could find. Her condition worsened, so I put a tube in the stump of the gall bladder and sewed her up. I told the family she was very seriously ill. We put her on intravenous feedings. The next morning she felt fine and was mad because they would not give her any breakfast. I tried to explain but she demanded food. We gave her some fat free liquids. She left the hospital on the twelfth day and remained well so far as I know. It just goes to show how a doctor cannot always know it all.

☆   ☆   ☆

I had one boy as a patient who was hit in the head with a ball bat. He became unconscious, then regained consciousness. Some two hours later he again became unconscious and was brought to the hospital, out like a light. His right pupil was larger than the left. His reflexes were not reliable. I thought of subarachnoid hemorrhage, bleeding between the brain and the skull. As I said before, in those days, if you needed something done, you did it. I took a few minutes in the library to see what the marks were for trephining for the middle meningeal artery. I trephined a hole about an inch in diameter. Here was a blood clot and after its removal there sat the middle meningeal artery squirting away. That is luck! I sutured it, put the trephined bone back in the hole and the boy got well. I haven't done one since and never had done one before.

☆   ☆   ☆

I had one good friend, a telephone operator, who was a lot of help. In the days when they plugged the telephone switchboard, Elsie would list my calls and call me when she knew I could talk, especially if I had been at the hospital all night. (She called me at home when the invasion of France started so my wife and I got up at 3:00 A.M. and were two of the early ones to know about it.) She would tell me where the call came from if I had been unable to answer the phone quickly enough. She is retired from Northwestern Bell Telephone Company now.

☆   ☆   ☆

One day my receptionist came into my consultation room, called me into the drug room, and said, "I believe a patient is dead in the reception room. He came in, sat down, took a deep breath and hasn't breathed since." I stepped out into the waiting room with ten or twelve people in it. I said, "This man has fainted. Will a couple of you men help me move him into my consultation room?" We did. I thanked the men and they returned to the waiting room. Yes, he was dead, sitting not over a foot from a patient. I tried to call his wife but couldn't locate her so called his daughter. With her consent, I had the undertaker come to my side hall, moved the man out on the cart, and down the stairs. No one knew the difference until they saw it in the papers. That is the only death in my office, thank goodness. Thanks to my office force it was handled very well.

☆   ☆   ☆

A call came from the hospital one day to come at once for an emergency. I went at once. Three boys, brothers, ages fifteen to eighteen or so, had been sawing logs and making 2 by 4 planks. The father ran this sawmill and had gone to town for some machinery. I noticed the right shoe of the younger boy was covered with blood. The nurses removed his clothing which was muddy and dirty and I took off his high top shoes. The boy's right foot below the shinbone was in the shoe, leaving the stump of the leg sticking out bare. The wound was cleaned, bleeders ligated. I talked to the older brothers. Such a stump was not the best for fitting an artificial foot. His foot had slipped and gone beneath the big saw. I wanted to amputate the leg below the knee to make a good stump. We could not locate the father or the mother. So I dressed the stump, gave tetanus toxoid and put the boy to bed. The two brothers were sent to find the parents. This was in the days before antibiotics. The father and the mother got to the hospital about 6:00 P.M. I talked to them, trying to be calm and patient. They didn't know me and I didn't know them. I explained as best I could about a good stump and the necessity of amputation. Today we would try sewing the foot back on. The parents refused to give consent and went home to think it over. They didn't believe much in doctors. The next morning they were at the hospital and stayed all day. They were fine people but a bit "woodsy."

The third day I walked into the room to dress the wound, I smelled the odor of gas gangrene. I had smelled that odor often in France in World War I. To save a life the extremity must be amputated above the joint. That meant in the midthigh. I had learned to know the people better now. They had begun to respect me. I explained that the amputation must be done at once so that the gas bacillus infection would not spread up between the layers of the muscle. Otherwise, the boy would die. The father would not talk. The mother was more understanding. I left them alone for a little while; then I went back to them and offered to send the boy to Iowa City or Mayo Clinic. They said, "No, we don't know them either." Then the mother said, "Doctor, we have faith in you. Do as you think best. Let's pray!" So we did. The boy was prepared for surgery and I amputated his right leg above the knee. He got along fine and the boy and his family became close friends to all in the hospital. An artificial leg was placed on the stump and he was taught to walk. That's not all. World War II came along. His brothers all enlisted. He couldn't, so he went to California and got a job at Lockheed where he stayed helping build airplanes for his brothers to fly in. After the war was over, he came to see me when he came home for a visit. He went to Gates Business College to learn bookkeeping, typing, etc. The next I saw him he had a wife and he owned a refrigerator locker and was planning more.

The father and mother, the sons, and a daughter adopted me as their doctor and advisor until they scattered over the country and built their own homes. The father decided that education was all right. His family had not been allowed to attend other than a country school. They had been expected to stay home and work on the bottom-land farm. The outlook of the entire family changed. The parents moved to Cedar Falls and lived there until they died. They were always grateful for the help I had given them. I have not seen the young man for some years.

☆   ☆   ☆

One morning I came in the door from the garage. The telephone was ringing. I got it on the first ring, "Yes, I'll be over shortly." I had just finished the busiest night ever in the hospital: three babies, one caesarean section, one appendectomy, a minor accident, and had admitted a lobar pneumonia patient. Just then "Ma" came down the stairs and said, "You have to go to bed." I ate a little breakfast and lay down for just a minute. I woke with a start, got up and dressed in a hurry, and went to that promised call. I knew them. The mother started telling me off about taking so long to make the call. "The child could be dead—it has been two and one-half hours since the call." I said nothing until I had looked at the child, then said, "If you are through bawling me out, I'll tell you that your child will be broken out with measles tomorrow, so please shut up." That is when I decided to write a book about *Unseen Battles of the Night*. Up until now, I never got started on anything, but guess this will be enough.

EPILOGUE

REMEMBER all those dictums—the past is prologue; you can't chart your future without knowing your past; without a sense of history you are bound to repeat past mistakes?

It is doubtful you were motivated—knowingly—by any of these admonitions as you browsed through these vignettes of some of our immediate ancestors. You probably read them for fun. But did they—perhaps unknowingly—arouse some misgivings about our present-day problems? Some of us, for example, feel buffeted about as we go spinning along in space and cry out, "Stop the world, I want to get off!" Or when we experience the complexity and confusion of our contemporary times we say, "Please, let us go back!"

But then we recall the family diet of cornbread mixed with water and corn coffee without cream or sugar which was the best that Asenath Gable could do. We remember the clashes between settlers and Indians. Or Bruce Siberts afoot in the Badlands in midwinter and only a quick rifle shot away from his last roundup.

So we pull back and say, well, let's not go to extremes; we just want the good parts of the Good Old Days.

But—they were all packaged together, the simple pleasure and the awful harshness.

And speaking of harshness, it must be borne in mind that these are stories of those who survived. Behind each survivor were those who succumbed to the rigors—who broke in spirit and in health, who were destroyed by the loneliness, the lack of medical care, and exertions beyond the limits of physical strength. Asenath Gable bore 11 children; how many women in that era must have given their lives for the birth of another. These thoughts, too, must be kept in mind as we recall these stories and try to put them—and ourselves—in some perspective.

In addition, these stories are another reminder of what a

211

remarkably young nation we are. These might well have been the experiences of some of our own grandparents or great-grandparents. Through them and their recollections we can reach out and—figuratively speaking—touch a good bit of all of American history. So much has happened so quickly that we shouldn't be all too sure of ourselves; we have no adequate background against which to measure our reactions.

So, aside from whatever vicarious pleasure we may have experienced from these stories of a bygone era, they may have—at least momentarily—helped us all to stand off and look at ourselves a little more closely as we relate to the accomplishments of those who came before us. Perhaps we can see our moment in history a little more clearly. In any case, a little serious self-appraisal, a little stocktaking, is a good thing for most of us; especially when it comes so pleasantly in the sugarcoated form of these snippets of pure nostalgia!

CARL HAMILTON